Islam Unveiled

The True Desert Storm

by Dr. Robert A. Morey

The Scholars Press
P.O. Box 290
Shermans Dale, PA 17090

Printed in the United States of America

Library Of Congress Card Catalog Number 91-061235

Morey, Robert A., 1946-
Islam Unveiled
Bibliography:

1. Islam. 2. Muhammad. 3. Allah. 4. The Quran
I. Title.

ISBN 0-9629394-0-4

The cover photo is of El Aqaba Mosque in Jordan
courtesy of Arab World Ministries.

About The Author

Dr. Morey is the Executive Director of the Research and Education Foundation and is the author of over twenty books some of which have been translated into French, German, Spanish, Italian, Finish, Polish and Chinese. He is an internationally recognized scholar in the field of comparative religions, the cults and the occult. The Research and Education Foundation is dedicated to investigating topics which affect Western culture and values.

For a catalogue of all of Dr. Morey's books and tapes, including his ten-part video series on Islam, write to:

The Research and Education Foundation
P.O. Box 141455
Austin, TX 78714

Table of Contents

Introduction

Islam is not only the dominant religion in the Middle East and North Africa but it is also the second largest religion in the world.

Western Europe

Indeed, due to liberal immigration policies, millions of Muslims have now emigrated to the West in search of a better life.

Thus in many Western "Christian" nations, Islam has become the second largest religion. For example, in France and Germany, the Muslims now number in the millions.

The United Kingdom

In England the situation is amazing. There are now more Arab Muslims in England than there are Methodists! There are even more Muslims than there are evangelical Christians.

Funded by the vast resources of Arab oil money, the Muslims are buying abandoned Anglican churches and turning them into Mosques at such a rate that some Muslims claim that England will be the first Muslim European country!

The legal situation has reached the point where the English Parliament has been forced to rule that Muslims do not have to follow English Common Law when it comes to such things as divorce. They can follow Islamic law instead.

Australia

Islam has grown from a mere 800 Muslims in 1955 to well over 200,000 by 1990. The influx of Arab immigrants is increasing at a steady rate.

In a lecture tour "down under" in the fall of 1990, we found large mosques in all the major cities.

North America

In North America, there are now over four million Muslims. Indeed, some researchers claim that there are now more Muslims than Jews in North America which would make Islam the second largest religion in the United States and Canada.

The United States

Over 500 Islamic centers have been built in the United States. Two thirds of American Muslims are of Arab descent while one third is composed of various black Muslim cults.

There are now officially more Muslims than Episcopalians in the United States. (1.)

Extravagant Claims

One word must be said about the extravagant claims made by some Muslims who say that there are as many as ten to twenty five million Muslims in the United States.

On Feb. 22, 1991, I was on a radio talk show with a representative of the Islamic Information Center of America. During the program he claimed that there were over two billion Muslims in the world and over ten million in the United States!

When I asked him for some kind of written documentation for these numbers, he did not provide any.

When I pointed out that the encyclopedias, almanacs, newspapers, and such magazines as Time, Newsweek, etc. estimate that there are only between three to four million Muslims in the U.S. and not ten million as he claimed, the Muslim representative responded by claiming that all the newspapers, encyclopedias, almanacs, magazines, etc., were wrong!

But as for us, we will stick with the standard reference works until the Muslims can come up with some kind of hard documentation. (2.)

For example, the 1989 Almanac states that there are only 2.6 million Muslims in North American and only 860 million Muslims world wide. (3.)

Even if we add a million to the total to bring us to 1991, this is still a far cry from Muslim claims.

One Muslim leader in Detroit, Mich. claimed on a radio program that there were over 600,000 Muslims in New York City alone! Such outlandish claims do their cause more harm than good.

But regardless of how many Muslims have immigrated to the West in search of employment, the host countries must try to understand and assimilate these newcomers to their shores.

Our Intent

We must state at the outset that it is not our intent in this book to offend devout Muslims. We are not trying to hurt their feelings or to embarrass them in any way.

We know from personal experience that many

Muslims are good, hard working people who have overcome impossible odds to make a new home for themselves in the West.

Freedom Of Religion

Yet, we know that many Muslims take personal offense at any criticism of their religious beliefs. They find it very difficult to understand that "freedom of religion" in the West means that people are free to criticize Islam as well as any other religion! This freedom is something that we jealously guard in the West.

This is sometimes very hard for Arab Muslims to understand because they previously lived in Islamic countries where any criticism of Muhammad or the Quran is viewed as a criminal offense punishable by death!

Under Islamic law no criticism of Islam is allowed. In other words, there is no freedom of or from religion in Muslim countries.

A Plea For Understanding

When Western scholars apply scientific standards to the truth claims of Islam, they do not want this to be construed as a personal attack on the motives or character of Muslims. The search for truth should never offend.

Indeed, an open and honest discussion of the differences between non-Muslims and Muslims can only serve to break down the walls of ignorance and prejudice.

No religion, no matter how fervently believed or zealously practiced, should be afraid of the searching light of scientific research.

The Gulf War

The recent war with Iraq revealed many things. Once Western troops were in the Middle East, Arab dictators such as Qaddaffi and Saddam Hussein called for a jihad, or Holy War, against these soldiers. Why?

A jihad was called on the sole basis that these soldiers are, by and large, professing Christians, and thus are considered infidels according to the Islamic faith. In other words, they called upon Muslims to kill these soldiers just because they are Christians. This is regrettable but true.

Religious Toleration

To the modern Western mind, religious differences should not lead to the destruction of the lives or property of anyone. People should be free to practice any or no religion according to the dictates of their own consciences.

This is why Muslims need to understand why Westerners sometimes feel uneasy about the mass migration of Arab Muslims into Europe and North America.

A Case In Point

USA TODAY on Feb. 6, 1991, placed on its first two pages the result of a survey it took of Arab Muslims living in the United States concerning their attitude toward the Allied war against Saddam Hussein. The results were startling.

When asked, "Are your willing to have your son or daughter fight for the United States in this war?", 82%

of American Arab Muslims said, "NO."

Thus only 18% of those surveyed were willing to back America in the war against Iraq!

When asked if they approved of the way President Bush was handling the situation, 62 % said, "NO."

The survey went on to state that over half of American Arab Muslims said that they would NOT support a U.S. war on any Arab nation!

Why This Attitude?

For all practical purposes, this survey revealed that Arab Muslims have not been assimilated into the melting pot of American culture. The survey would seem to indicate that they are still more Arab than American.

The Muslim attachment to Arab culture, Arab nations and Arab political causes even after living in the West for many years is what disturbs many Westerners.

They rightfully ask just where is the allegiance of Arab Muslims? Is it to the Western nations which have given them the opportunity for a better life? Or, is it still only to Arab nations?

Information Our Goal

It is our desire by this study to inform Western people as to the nature and claims of Islam and then to point out to them why solid scholarship has rejected those claims.

Sauce For The Gander and For the Goose

It must also be pointed out that Muslims do not hesitate to condemn and to contradict the essential doctrines of other religions such as Christianity.

After visiting various Muslim information centers and mosques, I have collected a vast amount of Muslim literature which openly attacks the Bible, denies the Trinity, the Deity of Christ, His Sonship, His death on the cross, His bodily resurrection, and His intercession at the right hand of God the Father. (4.)

Since Muslims evidently have no problem whatsoever in openly criticizing other religions, why should they have a problem with those who for good and sufficient reasons criticize Islam?

After all, the same Bill of Rights that guarantees to Muslims the freedom to criticize other religions also gives other people the freedom to criticize Islam. The sword of religious freedom always cuts both ways.

The Burden of Proof

The burden of proof in terms of Muhammad's call to be a prophet and the inspiration of the Quran is upon the Muslims. Thus we will be examining the arguments given by Muslims to see if, in fact, they hold up under careful scientific scrutiny.

One Last Note

We must also point out that there are spelling variations on key Arabic words. For example, the Arabian prophet's name has been spelled as Mohammed, Mohammad, Muhammed, and Muhammad. The sacred book of Islam has been spelled as Coran, Koran, Qo'ran, Qu'ron and Quran. The holy place in Mecca has been spelled as Kaaba, Ka'bah and Kabah.

In order to avoid confusion, we have adopted the spelling used in most scholarly works and journals on

Islam.

Footnotes

1. For estimates of three to four million Muslims in the United States see: Victor, Khalil and Deborah, Khalil, "When Muslims Meet Christians," (*Christian Herald*, July/Aug., 1988, pg. 45). Kent, Hart, "Da'wah and The Koran: Islam In America," (*Eternity*, vol. 39 (1988), no. 3, pgs. 5f). "Islam In America," (*U.S. News and World Report*, Oct., 8, 1990). Mimi, Hall, "Arab Americans Speak Out," (USA Today, Feb. 6, 1991, pg. 1.)

2. The program aired on Feb. 22, 1991 on radio station WHP in Harrisburg, Pa.

3. The 1989 Information Please Almanac, (Houghton Mifflin Company, Boston, 1989, p. 400.)

4. A good example of Muslim anti-Christian literature would be Maurice Bucaille's book, *The Bible, The Quran and Science*, (American Trust Pub., Indianapolis, Ind., 1979).

Part One

The Nature of Islam

1

A Modern Parable

Imagine, if you will, that one day during your lunch hour, as you were standing on a street corner minding your own business, a strangely dressed couple approached you and asked if they could speak to you for a moment.

The man was dressed with a powdered wig on his head, a silk shirt, a waistcoat, breeches that only reached to his knees, silk stockings and black shoes with a silver buckle on each shoe.

The woman had on a high powdered wig and a long flowing dress that reached almost to the ground. They looked like a couple that had just stepped out of a movie set for an American Revolutionary War film.

The couple began to explain to you that they were followers of a religion in which George Washington was a mighty prophet of Ba-al. Thus everything that George Washington taught, believed, said, and practiced must be accepted as the inspired word of Baal who is the one true God.

The speeches and letters which people think came from Washington are in the English language because that is the language of Heaven. Even though there are foreign language translations of some of these writings, they really cannot be understood unless they are read in the original English.

The speeches of Washington were actually written in Heaven on a tablet of stone. George Washington did not really write a single page of his works. They were given to him by the angel Gabriel out of Heaven. He merely recited them when Ba-al so ordered.

They went on to explain that, because he was a prophet of Ba-al, the true God, we must live as George Washington lived. For example, all men should dress in the manner in which George Washington dressed. All women in particular should adopt a dress that Mrs. Washington wore.

We must even eat the food that the Washingtons ate. For example, George Washington did not like peas. Thus no one should be allowed to eat peas today.

Washington's political views must be viewed as the only valid form of government. And, since he owned slaves, slavery must be viewed as being a valid political structure of today.

At that moment, the alarm on the man's wristwatch went off and he pulled a compass out of his coat pocket. After facing in a certain direction, the couple got down on their hands and knees and bowed in prayer.

After they had finished their prayers, they got up. You could not help but ask them what they were doing.

They responded that they had to pray five times a day toward Washington, D.C., where the Washington Memorial was built.

As a matter of fact, all those who were followers of

George Washington had to make a pilgrimage to Washington, D.C., at least once in their life time.

Once they got there, they had to run around the Washington Memorial seven times. Then they had to run down to the end of the mall and throw some stones at the devil.

The man and his wife also remarked that the Washington Memorial had actually been built by Adam. Although it had been subsequently destroyed at various periods, it had been rebuilt by Abraham and that all the biblical patriarchs actually lived at that exact spot. The Washington Memorial was a sacred site and it had always been part of the worship of God.

At this point, they asked for your opinion. You couldn't resist asking if this was Candid Camera, America's Funniest People, or some other show. They couldn't really be serious about this religion of Washingtonianism.

The idea of bowing in prayer toward the Washington Memorial was absurd. The memorial was not built by Adam or rebuilt by Abraham. The Patriarchs did not live in D.C. but in Israel. The whole thing was quite ridiculous.

They responded that they were in dead earnest and that they really believed that George Washington was a prophet of Ba-al and that his writings were the Word of God.

You responded by saying, "It seems to me that you have made a religion out of 18th century American colonial culture.

Do you really expect people at the end of the 20th century, to live, dress and eat in accordance with the habits and tastes of people living in the 1700s in the United States?

What if the Russians were to invent a religion in which we were told that we had to pray toward Moscow five times a day? Why can't the Japanese invent a religion in which everyone has to pray toward Tokyo? Why can't the Mexicans say that you must take a pilgrimage to Mexico City once in your lifetime or you will not be saved?

This whole religion seems to be silly at the least and racist at the worst. Why would you expect every culture and every race of people to live the way that people lived in 18th century colonial America? It simply doesn't make sense!"

At this point, the man opened his coat and revealed that he was wearing a shoulder harness with a gun in it. He said that his religion did not allow anyone to ridicule or blaspheme their holy faith.

At that moment, your wristwatch alarm went off, indicating that your lunch hour was over.

With a sigh of relief, you explained that you had to get back to work. But if they would like to talk with you further, they could meet you on this street corner sometime. With that said, you beat a hasty retreat without waiting for any response from them.

Conclusion

You had just encountered a religion which was actually the deification of 18th century colonial American culture.

It was actually more cultural than religious in essence. It was also a subtle form of racism in that it demanded that all men and women everywhere in the world should bow in prayer to the capital of the United States.

2

The Key to Islam

The modern parable that was presented in Chapter One may seem farfetched to the reader. But, in reality, it underscores the true essence of Islam.

Western people have such a difficult time comprehending Islam because they fail to understand that it is a form of cultural imperialism in which the religion and culture of 7th century Arabia are raised to the status of divine law.

Sacred vs Secular

Their difficulty in understanding Islam is rooted in the traditional Western philosophic concept of the separation of church and state.

In the West, organized religion is not viewed as having the power to rule over all of life. There is a secular realm in which organized religion has no authority.

Thus there is a "wall of separation" between church and state. For example, religious organizations in the West cannot set speed limits or legislate political laws.

But Islam cannot be simply viewed as one's private and personal religious preference. It is not just something you believe and then go on living as you please. There is no secular realm in Islamic countries.

Seventh Century Arabia

Islam is actually the "deification" of 7th century Arabian culture. In a very profound sense, Islam is more cultural than it is religious.

This is why all the textbooks and the encyclopedias of Islam begin with the historical context of Muhammad and the importance of 7th century Arabian culture.

Islam Is Arab Culture

Not too many years ago, I was invited to the home of a dear black Muslim friend who lived in New York City's famous Harlem section.

When I entered his apartment I found that even though they were born in the USA, they wore Arab clothing, listened to Arab music and ate Arab food! They even said a blessing over the food in Arabic although no one in the family knew the language.

They had abandoned American culture and adopted Arabian culture instead. This is what Islam meant to them.

No, we are NOT saying that Arab culture is "bad" just because it is Arab anymore than we would say that American culture is "good" just because it is American. All cultures have their good and bad points.

As a matter of fact, it was wrong for Westerners in the past to assume that their culture should be imposed upon the rest of the world. When it comes down to it, Western cultural imperialism is as bad as Arab cultural imperialism.

What disturbs Middle East scholars is that the Arabs have gone one step further. They have taken 7th Century Arabian culture and turned it into a religion.

Dr. Arthur Arberry
The most reliable English translation of the Quran in our opinion was done by Dr. Arthur J. Arberry who was the Head of Middle Eastern Studies at Cambridge University and an outstanding professor of Arabic and Persian.

In his famous two volume work, *Religion In the Middle East,* Prof. Arberry states that Islam is a "peculiarly Arabian religion" because, Islam, "as a religion and a culture we recognize as fundamentally one." [1]

Even Muslim scholars such as Dr. Ali Dashti, a past Foreign Minister of Iran, in his book, *Twenty Three Years: A Study Of The Prophetic Career Of Mohammad,* carefully documents how Islam must be understood in terms of its essential identification with 7th century Arab culture.

Religion In The West
This can be hard for Westerners to understand because religion in the West is viewed as something that is intensely personal and private and not a cultural phenomenon.

For example, Christianity does not demand that people today should dress in accordance with first century dress codes. Or, that they can eat only what Jesus ate.

Christianity is thus "supra-cultural" in that it allows people to live, dress and eat in accordance with the culture in which they are living.

But this is not so with Islam. Whenever Islam becomes the dominant religion in a country, it alters the culture of that nation and transforms it into the culture of 7th century Arabia.

This is why it is so hard for Muslims to convert to another religion. Every aspect of life has been dictated by Islam. The Muslim must follow the dictates of Islam, regardless of where he lives or what he thinks about it.

No Secular Realm

Thus to the Muslim, there is no "secular" realm where he is free from Islam. To the devout Muslim, Islam is all of life. As Kerry Lovering correctly pointed out, "Islam is a total way of life, not just a religion." [2]

In Islam there is no "separation of Mosque and state" that compares to the "separation of church and state" that prevails in most Western countries. Islamic religion and politics are one.

As Egyptian born Victor Kahlil points out,

> Islam regulates every aspect of life, to the point that culture, religion and politics in a Muslim country are practically inseparable. [3]

Muhammad took the Arab culture around him with all of its secular and sacred customs and made it into the religion of Islam.

Arab Racism

Thus Islam is fueled by a subtle form of racism in which 7th century Arabian culture in its political expression, family affairs, dietary laws, clothing, religious rites, language, etc., are to be imposed on all other cultures.

The Ishmael Myth

One example of Arab racism is the myth that the Arabs are the descendants of Abraham through his son Ishmael. This claim was made in response to the Jews who had boasted that Abraham was the father of their race. (4.)

McClintock and Strong's well known encyclopedia on religion comments,

> There is a prevalent notion that the Arabs, both of the south and north, are descended from Ishmael; and the passage in Gen. xvi:12 . . . is often cited as if it were a prediction of that national independence which, upon the whole, the Arabs have maintained more than any other people. But this supposition (in so far as the true meaning of the text quoted is concerned) is founded on a misconception of the original Hebrew . . .These prophecies found their accomplishment in the fact of the sons of Ishmael being located, generally speaking, to the east of the other descendants of Abraham, whether by Sara or by Keturah. But the idea of the southern Arabs being of the posterity of Ishmael is entirely without foundation, and seems to have originated in the tradition invented by Arab vanity that they, as well as the Jews, are of the seed of Abraham - a vanity which, besides disfiguring and falsifying the whole history of the patriarch and his son Ishmael, has transferred the scene of it from Palestine to Mecca . . . the vast tracts of country known to us under the name of Arabia gradually became peopled by a variety of tribes of different lineage. [5]

Most standard reference works on Islam reject the Arab claim to Abrahamic descent. The prestigious Encyclopedia of Islam traces the Arabs to non-Abrahamic origins.[6] Even The Dictionary of Islam questions the whole idea that the Arabs are descendants of Ishmael.[7]

A Radio Debate

During a radio talk show in Feb. of 1991, I made the comment that the Arabs were not the descendants of Abraham. An American black Muslim called into the show to disagree with my viewpoint. He stated emphatically that the Arabs were indeed descended from Ishmael.

When I asked him for proof, all he could come up with was that he had been told by some Arab friends that this was so. Needless to say, I was not impressed by his "proof."

I then asked him if the Arabs of the Middle East were all the descendants of Abraham, whatever happened to the all the Akkadians, Summarians, Assyrians, Babylonians, Persians, Egyptians, Hittites, etc. that lived before, during and after Abraham? What happened to all those millions of people who were not Abraham's descendants? Where did they go? To this he could give no reply.

A Religious Reason

The compelling reason why Muslims claim to be descendants of Abraham is a religious one. The Quran transfers the historical setting of the biblical Patriarchs from Palestine to Mecca. The Quran even has Abraham rebuilding the Kabah!

If it be admitted that Abraham never lived in Mecca and thus the Arabs are not his descendants, then the Quran itself would be overturned.

Yet, the archeological evidence is overwhelming that Abraham never lived in Mecca! He came from the city of Ur which has been found in Iraq. He then moved West to Palestine from there. [8]

The following examples will demonstrate beyond all doubt the cultural nature of Islam.

Arab Islamic Law

First, Muhammad took the political laws which governed 7th century Arabian tribes and made them into the laws of Allah.

In such tribes, the sheik, or chief, had absolute authority over those under him. There was no concept of civil or personal rights in 7th century Arabia. The head of the tribe decided whether you lived or died.

This is why Islamic countries are always inevitably ruled by dictators or "strong men" who rule as despots. There are 21 Arab nations and not one of them is a democracy. Why is this?

Why No Democracy?

Democracy has never flourished in Arab nations because of the religion of Islam. Thus the more "secular" an Arab nation becomes, the more "democratic" it becomes. The highly secularized Egypt is an example.

But whenever Islamic fundamentalism regains dominance, the nation is plunged back into the "dark ages" of 7th century Arabia. Iran is a recent example of what happens to a nation when Islamic fundamentalism takes over the government.

The despots of the Ottoman Empire, and the dictators of Libya, Jordan, Iran, Iraq, Syria, Sudan, Yemen, etc., are merely examples of 7th century Arabian tyranny.

Civil Rights

Secondly, because there was no concept of personal freedom or civil rights in the tribal life of 7th century Arabia, Islamic law does not recognize freedom of speech, freedom of religion, freedom of assembly, or the freedom of the press. This is why non-Muslims, such as Christians or the Bahais, are routinely denied even the most basic civil rights.

In the West, people are free to protest what their government is doing. This is why thousands of people were even allowed to protest the Allied war against Iraq. They had the freedom of speech and assembly to do so.

But what if they lived in an Islamic country such as Saudi Arabia? There was no freedom to protest the war in Saudi Arabia. The Associated Press reported on Feb. 2, 1991, that,

> Prince Nazef had warned that anyone undermining the kingdom's security would be executed or have a hand and a leg cut off. [9]

Those who protested the war in the West did not even get a traffic ticket much less a leg or hand cut off!

Praying Toward Mecca

Thirdly, a Muslim is required to pray five times a day. This, in and of itself, is not offensive. It is good for a man to pray.

However, the Muslim is told that he must pray

toward Mecca, which is in Saudi Arabia, five times a day. Thus, he is reminded five times a day that he must bow in obedience to Arabia.

What if there was a Russian religion that required us to bow five times toward Moscow? What about the religion of Washingtonianism which said that we must bow five times a day towards Washington, D.C. Or, a Japanese religion that would require us to bow toward Tokyo?

The act of bowing in prayer five times a day toward Arabia is merely a symptom of the underlying cultural imperialism that lies at the heart of Islam.

Pilgrimage To Mecca

Fourthly, a Muslim is required, despite the hardship and great cost, to make a pilgrimage to Saudi Arabia to worship at the Kabah in Mecca at least once in his lifetime.

Imagine if a Russian religion demanded that once in your lifetime you had to travel to Moscow and worship at Red Square. Or, that an American religion demanded that you had to travel to the Washington Memorial in the United States.

The historical evidence is crystal clear that Muhammad adopted the pagan religious rite of a pilgrimage to Mecca to worship at the Kabah in order to appease the Meccan merchants who made a tremendous amount of money out of these pilgrimages. Thus for financial and cultural reasons, Islam adopted the pagan pilgrimage to Mecca. [10]

This pilgrimage has been both cruel and unnecessary and has fostered great hardship upon poor third-world Muslims who have to skimp and save their entire lives in order to fulfill this "pillar" of Islam. It makes no more sense than making a pilgrimage to Washington, D.C. or Moscow.

Dietary Laws

Fifthly, what foods were acceptable and not acceptable in 7th century Arabia are now mandated by Islam for all people. Thus what Muhammad ate and did not eat is made to be a divine law for all people.

The Woman's Veil

Sixthly, what an illiterate, nomadic tribeswoman wore in the desert of 7th century Arabia is mandated by Islam as the dress code for Muslim women today in every nation.

To be covered from head to foot to protect yourself from the desert sun is both practical and understandable if you are living in a desert. Arabian women dressed that way long before Muhammad was ever born. But to impose such desert garb on women everywhere is a form of cultural imperialism.

Women's Rights

Seventhly, the oppressive nature of Islam is seen most clearly in its denial of basic civil rights to women. The well known Muslim scholar Ali Dashti states,

In pre-Islamic Arab society, the women did not have the status of independent persons, but were considered to be possessions of the men. All sorts of inhumane treatment of the women were permissible and customary.[11]

The Quran states in Sura 4:34,

Men are the managers of the affairs of women...those

you fear may be rebellious - admonish; banish them to their couches and beat them.

The Arabic is much stronger than the word "beat them." It actually says "scourge them." Mohammed Pickthall correctly translates it this way in his version of the Quran.

Again, Dashti comments,

The statement that "men are the guardians of women" in verse 38 of sura 4 postulates inequality of men and women in civil rights. The words are followed by two brief explanations of men's superiority over women.[12]
In Islamic law, male heirs get more than female heirs, and men's evidence is more reliable than women's; to be exact, a man's inheritance share is twice a woman's share, and his evidence carries twice the weight of hers in court . . .The right to divorce belongs to the husband but not to wives. [13]

From time to time we will quote from Muslim scholars such as Ali Dashti to demonstrate that Western scholars are not operating out of a hidden bias against Islam. Their findings are supported by recognized Muslim and non-Muslim authorities in the field of Middle East Studies.

The denial of civil rights to women which is clearly in the text of the Quran itself is reflective of 7th century Arabian culture and its low view of women.

Even today, Muslim women can be kept prisoners in their own homes. They can even be denied the right to go outside the house if the husband so orders. They are even still denied the right to vote in many Islamic countries such as Kuwait!

In Islamic countries such as Iran, women must carry written permission from their husbands to be out of the house! Women are even denied the right to drive a car in such places as Saudi Arabia.

A Recent Case In Point

On March 10, 1991, the New York Times Magazine, (pgs 26-46), reported the following story on women's rights in Saudi Arabia.

> The crisis in the gulf last fall spawned a messy and much publicized demonstration by women, who dumped their chauffeurs and drove in convoy, defying an informal ban on driving by women. The incident prompted a vicious campaign against them by religious fanatics, with Government acquiescence. Underlying these strains is the question of how much power the religious establishment should have, in particular the religious police, or mutawwa.

> They patrol the streets and shopping malls, telling women to cover their faces and young men to pray. The only people with spine in this society are the 47 women who drove, one Saudi intellectual said, "And look what happened to them. They were thrown to the wolves." The Government punished them as severely as it would any public protesters. Virtually all of those who taught at one university were dismissed by order of the King. The women, as well as their husbands and even some of their relatives, were forbidden to leave the kingdom. They were ordered not to meet with Western reporters or to discuss their situation with any outsider, and they were

warned of further reprisals if they attempted to drive again or stage another demonstration.

But the Government's abuse of these women was mild compared with their treatment by the religious establishment . . . the fundamental sheiks denounced them from one of the kingdom's most powerful political platforms, the mosque pulpits. In Friday sermons after the protest, the women were branded as "red communists," "dirty American secularists," "whores and prostitutes," "fallen women," and "advocates of vice." Their names, occupations, addresses and phone numbers were. . . . distributed in leaflets around the mosque and other public places. One leaflet accused them of having renounced Islam, an offense punishable by death in Saudi Arabia. Several of the women remained unrepentant, convinced that eventually the issue of the their status will be addressed. "The issue is not driving," one of them said. "It is that here in Saudi Arabia, I exist as a person from the bellybutton to the knees."

Cruel And Unusual Punishment

Eighthly, incarceration without due process, the use of torture, political assassination, the cutting off of hands, feet, ears, tongues, heads, and the gouging out of eyes - all of these things are part of Islamic law today because they were part of 7th century Arabian culture. [14]

To Westerners, such things are barbaric and have no place in the modern world.

Conclusion

Islam is a distinctively Arabian cultural religion. Unless this is firmly grasped, no real understanding of

Islam is possible. Unless this fundamental point is understood, Western people will never understand why Muslims think and act the way they do.

Footnotes

1. Arthur, J., Arberry, Religion In The Middle East, (Cambridge University Press, London, 1969), II:3.

2. Kerry, Lovering, "Mecca Challenges The World," (Africa Now, Sudan Interior Mission, Jan./Feb., 1979) p. 39.

3. Victor, Khalil and Deborah, Khalil, ibid., p. 43.

4. The Concise Dictionary Of Islam, ed. Cyril Classe, (Stacey Inter., London, 1989), p. 179.

5. John, McClintock and James, Strong, Cyclopedia of Biblical, Theological, and Ecclesiastical Literature, (Baker Book House, Grand Rapids, 1981 reprint), I:339.

6. The Encyclopedia of Islam, ed. Gibb, Levi-Provencial, Schacht, (J. Brill, Leiden, 1913), I:543-547.

7. Thomas, Hughes, A Dictionary of Islam, (Allen & Co., London, 1885) pp.18f.

8. J. A., Thompson, The Bible And Archeology, (Wm. B. Eerdmans Pub. Co., Grand Rapids, 1965) pgs. 13-36.

9. Quoted in the Harrisburg Patriot News, Feb. 6, 1991, p. A 3.

10. Ali, Dashti, 23 Years: A Study Of The Prophetic Career Of Mohammad, (George Allen & Unwin, London, 1985) pgs. 33-38.

11. ibid., p. 113.

12. ibid., p. 113.

13. ibid., p. 114

14. ibid., p. 56.

Part Two

The Cultural Background of Islam

3

Pre-Islamic Arabia

Since the faith of Islam would deem it blasphemous to even suggest that the teachings of Muhammad and the Quran find their source in earthly pre-Islamic custom, culture, and religion, Muslims did not do any significant research on what pre-Islamic Arabia was like.

It was thus left to Western scholars since the turn of the century to discover the cultural and literary sources that Muhammad used in the construction of his religion and of the Quran itself.

This is why every Western reference work on Islam begins with a section on pre-Islamic Arabia and its influence on the teachings and religious rites of Muhammad. The historical background of Islam cannot be ignored.

Indeed, if sources for Islam can be found in pre-Islamic Arabian culture, custom, and religion, then the doctrine that Muhammad's faith and the Quran were brought down from Heaven and do not have any earthly human origin would be at stake.

Circular Reasoning

Muslims frequently argue in a circle at this point. They argue that since the faith of Islam and the Quran were sent down out of Heaven, there can be no earthly sources or materials that were used in their construction. Thus they begin with the assumption that such things cannot be.

But Western scholarship cannot make such a gratuitous assumption. As we shall see, the Islamic faith and the Quran itself can be completely and sufficiently explained in terms of pre-Islamic Arabian culture, custom, and religion.

Special attention should be made to the pioneering work of Julius Wellhausen, Theodor Noldeke, Joseph Halevy, Edward Glaser, William F. Albright, Frank P. Albright, Richard Bell, J. Arberry, Wendell Phillips, W. Montgomery Watt, Alfred Guillaume, Arthur Jeffery, etc.

The archeological and linguistic work that has been done since the later part of the 19th century has unearthed overwhelming evidence that Muhammad constructed his religion and the Quran from pre-existing material in Arabian culture.

The Meaning Of Islam

For example, the very word "Islam" is not a word that was revealed from heaven or invented by Muhammad. It is an Arabic word which originally referred to the attribute of manliness in which one would be heroic and brave in battle even unto death.

The Middle East scholar, Dr. M. Bravmann, documents in his fascinating work, The Spiritual Background of Early Islam, that the word "islam" originally meant, a secular concept, denoting a sublime virtue in the eyes of the primitive Arab; defiance of death, heroism; to die in battle.[1]

Islam did not originally mean "submission." Instead, it referred to that strong attribute that characterized a desert warrior who, even when faced with impossible odds, would fight unto death for his tribe. The word Islam slowly developed into the meaning of "submission" as Dr. Jane Smith at Harvard University has demonstrated.[2]

Pre-Islamic Tribal Life

The tribal society aspect of pre-Islamic Arabia explains many of the things that can be found in Islam today.

The tribes were constantly at war with one another. But these wars did not involve a great loss of life because the weapons were quite primitive.

It was felt that it was perfectly in line with morality to mount raids on other tribes in order to obtain wealth, wives, and slaves. These desert tribes lived by the code of "an eye for an eye and a tooth for a tooth." Vengeance was extracted whenever anything was done to hurt any member of the tribe.

There was a harsh penal code that was followed by the nomadic Arabian tribes. It meant nothing to them to cut off the right hand, a foot or the head of someone. The tongue could be cut out, the ears lobbed off, and even the eyes gouged out as punishment for various crimes. To sneak up behind someone and slit his throat from ear to ear was viewed as as the right thing to do in certain situations and the person who did it was viewed as a hero.

Forcing people into slavery, kidnapping women and then holding them in your harem and raping them at will was considered just and proper. The harsh Arabian climate produced a harsh tribal society in which violence was the norm. This is why violence is still an unhappy attribute of Islamic societies.

A Modern Example

The desperate plight of Salman Rushdie is a modern example of Arab violence.

To receive a death sentence for writing a book which gives an unfavorable view of Muhammad is something a Westerner can neither understand or tolerate. But to an Arab Muslim, it makes perfect sense. Dr. William Montgomery Watt of Edinburgh University stated,

> It should be emphasized that the Arabs did not regard killing a person as in itself wrong. It was wrong if the person was a member of your kin-group or an allied group; and in Islam this meant the killing of any believer (4:92). Out of fear of retaliation one did not kill a member of a strong tribe. In other cases, however, there was no reason for not killing.[3]

In the United States, the black Muslim movement has had a particularly ugly history of violence. This violence has included assassinating their own leaders.

The Assassins

It is interesting to note that the English word "assassin" is actually an Arabic word! It comes from the Latin word "assassinus" which is taken from the Arabic word "hashahashin."

"Hashahashin" literally means, "smokers of hash-ish" and was used as a description of those Muslims who smoked hashish to whip themselves into a religious frenzy before killing their enemies.

It came into European vocabulary through the Muslim sect called "The Assassins" who believed that Allah had called them to kill people as a sacred duty.

The Assassins terrorized the Middle East from the 11th to the 13th century and even made the Western explorer Marco Polo fear for his life.[4]

The Quran and Violence

This should not surprise anyone because Islam not only condones such violence but actually commands it in certain instances.

In the Quran, Muslims are told in Sura 9:5,

> Fight and slay the pagans (i.e. infidels) wherever ye find them, and seize them, beleaguer them, and lie in wait for them in every stratagem of war.

What are Muslims supposed to do to the people who resist Islam? Sura 5:33 says that,

> Their punishment is . . . execution, or crucifixion, or the cutting off of hands and feet from the opposite sides, or exile from the land.

In the modern West such things as cutting off someone's hands or legs because he will not accept your religion is no longer acceptable. The horrors of the Inquisition serve as warning to all what fanatics can do.

The City of Mecca

Secondly, it needs to be pointed out that Mecca was in the control of the Quraysh tribe into which Muhammad was born. Mecca was also the dominant religious center for all the pagan religions in Arabia. Chamber's Encyclopedia points out that,

> The community in which Mohammed grew up was pagan, different localities having their own gods, often represented by stones. In many places there were sanctuaries to which pilgrimage was made. Mecca contained one of the most important, the Kaaba, in which was placed the black stone, long an object of worship.[5]

Archeologists have unearthed many examples of pre-Islamic art which includes their idols and symbols of worship.[6]

As the Encyclopedia Britannica points outs, the financial base of the Quraysh tribe depended upon the caravans and the trade routes that would particularly go through Mecca in order for pagans of all stripes to worship their particular idol at the Kabah.[7]

The Kabah

The Quraysh tribe had seen to it that there was an idol for every religion at a pagan temple called the Kabah. It was a virtual smorgasbord of deities with something for everyone.

The word "Kabah" is the Arabic word for cube and refers to the square stone temple in Mecca where the idols were worshipped. At least 360 gods were represented at the Kabah and a new one could be added if some stranger came into town and wanted to worship his own god in addition to the ones that were already represented at the Kabah.

The lucrative trade routes and the rich caravans formed the cultural link between Africa, the Middle East, the East, and the West. Thus, it is no surprise to find stories in the Quran whose origin can be traced back to Egypt, Babylon, Persia, India, and even to Greece.

Magic and the Genies

In terms of pre-Islamic religious life, the basic orientation of the people was that of superstition. The Arabs believed in the "evil eye," the casting of curses and spells, magic stones, fatalism, fetishes, and the fabulous stories of the jinns, or, what we call genies or fairies.

Most people in their childhood read the fantastic fables found in the "Arabian Nights" such as the genie in Aladdin's Lamp, flying carpets, etc.

It is no surprise therefore to find that the Quran contains references to such things as the evil eye, curses, fatalism, and the fabulous jinns. (Suras 55; 72; 113 and 114). [8]

In some Islamic countries, many Muslims still wear an amulet around the neck in which a part of the Quran is recorded to ward off the "evil eye."

Animistic Religion

Secondly, the population was basically animistic in orientation. The male and female jinns, or spirits, which lived in trees, stones, rivers and in mountains were worshipped and feared by the Arabs.

There were tribal or sacred magic stones and these stones were said to protect the tribe. The Quraysh tribe had adopted a black stone as their tribal magic stone and had set it up at the Kabah. This magical black stone was kissed when people came on their pilgrimage to worship at the Kabah. It was no doubt an asteroid that had fallen out of the sky and thus was viewed as being divine in some way.[9]

The Sabeans

Thirdly, the dominant religion that had grown very powerful just before Muhammad's time was that of the Sebean's.

The Sebeans had an astral religion in that they worshipped the heavenly bodies. The moon was viewed as a male deity and the sun as the female deity. Together they produced other deities such as the stars. The Quran refers to this in Sura 41:37 and elsewhere.

They used a lunar calendar to regulate their religious rites. For example, a month of fasting was regulated by the phases of the moon. The Sabean pagan rite of fasting began with the appearance of a crescent moon and did not cease until the crescent moon reappeared. [10] This would later be adopted as one of Islam's five pillars.

Pagan Rites

The fourth thing that contributed to the religious world into which Muhammad was born was that of pagan ritualism.

The pagans of pre-Islamic Arabia taught that everyone should bow and pray toward Mecca at certain set times during the day. Everyone should also make a pilgrimage to Mecca to worship at the Kabah at least once in his life.

Once they arrived at Mecca, the pagans ran around the Kabah seven times, kissed the black stone and then ran about a mile to the Wadi Mina to throw stones at the devil.

They also believed in the giving of alms and the condemnation of usury. They even had a certain month in which fasting was to be done according to the lunar calendar.[11]

That these pagan rites comprised the religion in which Muhammad was raised by his family is acknowledged by all. Thus it is no surprise to find that, as the Arab scholar Nazar-Ali pointed out, "Islam retained many aspects of pagan religion." [12]

Alfred Gullaume, who was Head of the Department of The Near and Middle East School of Oriental Studies and Professor of Arabic at the University of London, and later taught at Princeton University, comments, "The customs of heathenism have left an indelible mark on Islam, notably in the rites of the pilgrimage."[13]

Prof. Augustus H. Strong stated that Islam, "is heathenism in monotheistic form."[14]

Foreign Religions

Fifthly, the influence of foreign religions was also felt in pre-Islamic Arabia.

The Jews

The Jews in large numbers had moved into Arabia and had grown very wealthy not only in trade but also in the gold and silver business. Stories from the Old Testament, the Misnah, the Talmud, and Jewish apoc-

ryphal works such as the Testament of Abraham were
well known in pre-Islamic Arabia.

The Zoroasterians

There was also the influence of the Zoroastrian
religion. Traders from Persia frequently passed through
Mecca telling their favorite fables.

Because the main trade route went through Mecca,
people from Eastern lands such as India and China also
spread their religious ideas and stories in Arabia.

It is no surprise to find in the Quran itself remnants
of religious stories that can be ultimately traced back to
Hinduism, Buddhism, Mythraism, Greek Mystery
religions, and of course, the Egyptian religions.

The Christians

Christianity had already been introduced into south-
ern Arabia and was flourishing there by the time
Muhammad was born.

But the Christianity that was present in Arabia was
in an uneducated and garbled form and, worse yet,
sometimes heretical in nature.

Some of the heretical teachings of the Gnostics were
present in pre-Islamic Arabia in such fraudulent
"Gospels" as "The Gospel of Barnabas." These Gnostic "gospels" began to appear in the later part of the 3rd
century and reached their highest influence during the
4th through the 7th centuries. Their presence in pre-
Islamic Arabia is well known.

Conclusion

The religious ideas and rites found in Islam and the
Quran can be traced back to pre-Islamic culture, cus-

tom, and religious life.

Western scholars came to this conclusion when they asked such questions as, "Why does the Quran NEVER explain its ideas or rites? Why does it NEVER define the meaning of such words as Allah, Islam, Mecca, jinn, pilgrimage, Kabah, etc.?"

The only rational conclusion one can come to is that the Quran does not explain such terminology because Muhammad assumed that whoever read the Quran would already be familiar with pre-Islamic culture, custom, and religious life.

This is why the Quran never explains the identity of the people mentioned in its many stories. It is assumed that the reader would already be familiar with these stories from pre-Islamic sources. Thus no explanation was needed.

We are aware that these kinds of questions and the historical research that they generated pose a serious threat to the religion of Islam which teaches that the Quran literally came down from heaven and thus cannot have any earthly author or sources.

We understand the agony of Muslims at this issue. They are in a tight spot. In an attempt to save the Quran, they could admit that Muhammad and not Allah was its author and that it was written on earth and not in heaven as it claims. This would explain all the pre-Islamic material in the Quran.

But in their attempt to save the Quran, they have actually guaranteed its destruction. In the end, the Muslim must give up his belief in the heavenly origin of the Quran. If this is done, Islam cannot stand.

Footnotes

1. M., Bravmann, The Spiritual Background of Early Islam, (E. J. Brill, Leiden, 1972).

2. Jane, Smith, An Historical and Semetic Study of the Term Islam As Seen In A Sequence of Quran Commentaries, (University of Montana Press, for Harvard University Dissertations, 1970).

3. William, Montgomery, Watt, Muhammad's Mecca, (Edinburgh University Press, Edinburgh, 1988), pgs. 18-19.

4. For the fullest account of this group, see: Marshall, Hodgson, The Order Of Assassins, (Mouton & Co., Gravenhage, 1955).

5. Chamber's Encyclopedia, (International Learning Center, London, 1973) IX:453.

6.Praeger Encyclopedia of Art, (Prager Pub., N.Y., 1971),pp.68-70. Encyclopedia of World Art, (McGraw-Hill Book Co., N.Y., 1959) I:537f.

7. The Encyclopedia Britannica, ibid., 15:150f.

8. Besides the standard references to "jinn" in Islamic dictionaries and encyclopedias, see Dashti and Bravmann for two particularly enlightening discussions.

9. Nearly all Western reference works have a section on the pre-Islamic history of Mecca, the Kabah and the black stone. For example see the Encyclopedia Britannica, 15:150f; The Encyclopedia of Religion (ed. Eliade) 8:225f; The International Standard Bible Encyclopedia, I:218; etc.

10. For further information on the Sabeans, see: The Encyclopedia of Religion, (ed. Eliade), ibid., 1:364-365; 7:303; 8:225f.

4

The Cult of the Moon-God

It will come as a surprise to many Westerners that the word "Allah" was not something invented by Muhammad or revealed for the first time in the Quran.

The well known Middle Eastern scholar H. Gibb, pointed out that the reason that Muhammad never had to explain who "Allah" was in the Quran was that his listeners had already heard about Allah long before Muhammad was ever born.[1]

Dr. Arthur Jeffery, who was one of the foremost Western Islamic scholars in modern times and Professor of Islamic and Middle East Studies at Columbia University, pointed out that,

> The name Allah, as the Quran itself is witness, was well known in pre-Islamic Arabia. Indeed, both it and its feminine form, Allat, are found not infrequently among the theophorous names in inscriptions from North Africa.[2]

The word Allah comes from the compound Arabic word, al-ilah. The "al" is the definite article "the" and the word "ilah" is an Arabic word for "god." It is not a foreign word. It was not even the Syriac word for God. It is pure Arabic.[3]

Neither is "Allah" a Hebrew or Greek word for God as found in the Bible. Allah is an Arabic term used in reference to an Arabian deity.

Hastings' Encyclopedia of Religion and Ethics states,

"Allah" is a proper name, applicable only to their (i.e. Arab) peculiar God.[4]

According to the Encyclopedia of Religion,

"Allah" is a pre-Islamic name . . . corresponding to the Babylonian Bel.[5]

Due to past experiences with recalcitrant students who found it hard to believe that "Allah" was a pagan name for a peculiar pagan Arabian deity in pre-Islamic times, the following citations are given.

Allah is found...in Arabic inscriptions prior to Islam. (Encyclopedia Britannica)[6]

The Arabs, before the time of Mohammed, accepted and worshipped, after a fashion, a supreme god called allah. (The Encyclopedia of Islam, ed. Houtsma)[7]

Allah was known to the pre-Islamic Arabs; he was one of the Meccan deities. (Encyclopedia of Islam, ed. Gibb)[8]

ilah . . . appears in pre-Islamic poetry . . . By frequency of usage, al-ilah was contracted to allah, frequently attested to in pre-Islamic poetry. (The Encyclopedia of Islam, ed. Lewis)[9]

The name Allah goes back before Muhammed. (Encyclopedia of World Mythology And Legend)[10]

The origin of this (Allah) goes back to pre-Muslim times. Allah is not a common name meaning "God" (or a "god"), and the Muslim must use another word or form if he wishes to indicate any other than his own peculiar deity. (Encyclopedia Of Religion and Ethics)[11]

To the testimony of the above standard reference works, we add those of such scholars as Henry Preserved Smith of Harvard University who said,

Allah was already known by name to the Arabs.[12]

Dr. Kenneth Cragg, who was the editor of the prestigious scholarly journal "Muslim World" and an outstanding modern Western Islamic scholar, whose works were generally published by Oxford University, comments,

The name Allah is also evident in archeological and literary remains of pre-Islamic Arabia.[13]

Dr. W. Montgomery Watt, who was Professor of Arabic and Islamic Studies at Edinburgh University and Visiting Professor of Islamic studies at College de France, Georgetown University and the University of Toronto, has done extensive work on the pre-Islamic concept of Allah. He concludes that,

In recent years I have become increasingly convinced that for an adequate understanding of the career of Muhammad and the origins of Islam, great importance must be attached to the existence in Mecca of belief in Allah as a "high god." In a sense this is a form of paganism, but it is so different from paganism as commonly understood that it deserves separate treatment.[14]

Caesar Farah in his book on Islam concludes his discussion of the pre-Islamic meaning of Allah by saying,

There is no reason, therefore, to accept the idea that Allah passed to the Muslims from the Christians and Jews.[15]

According to Middle East scholar E. M. Wherry, whose translation of the Quran is still used today, in pre-Islamic times, Allah-worship, as well as Baal-worship, were both astral religions in that they involved the worship of the sun, the moon and the stars.[16]

Astral Religions

In Arabia, the sun god was viewed as a female goddess and the moon as the male god. As has been pointed out by many scholars such as Alfred Guilluame, the moon god was called by various names, one of which was Allah![17]

The name Allah was used as the personal name of the moon god versus other titles that could be given to him.

Allah, the moon god, was married to the sun-goddess. Together they produced three goddesses who were called "the daughters of Allah." These three goddesses were called Al-Lat, Al-Uzza, and Manat.

The "daughters of Allah," along with Allah and the sun-goddesses were viewed as "high" gods. That is, they were viewed as being at the top of the pantheon of Arabian deities. Along with Allah, however, they worshipped a host of lesser gods and "daughters of Allah."[18]

The Crescent Moon Symbol

The symbol of the worship of the moon god in Arabian culture and elsewhere throughout the Middle East was the crescent moon.

Archeologists have dug up numerous statues and hieroglyphic inscriptions in which a crescent moon was seated on top of the head of the deity to symbolize the worship of the moon god.

The Gods Of The Quraysh

The Quraysh tribe into which Muhammad was born was particularly devoted to Allah, the moon god and especially to Allah's three daughters who were viewed as intercessors between them and Allah.

The worship of the three goddesses, Al-Lat, Al-Uzza, and Manat played a significant role in the worship at the Kabah in Mecca. The first two daughters of Allah had names which were feminine forms of Allah.

The literal Arabic name of Muhammad's father was Abd-Allah. His uncle's name was literally Obied-Allah. Thus the very names of his father and his uncle revealed the personal devotion that Muhammad's pagan family had to the worship of Allah, the moon god.

Praying Toward Mecca

An Allah idol was set up at the Kabah along with all the other idols. The pagans prayed toward Mecca and the Kabah because that is where their gods were stationed.

It only made sense to them to face in the direction of their gods and then pray. Since the idols of their god were at Mecca, they prayed toward Mecca.

The worship of the moon god was far greater than the Allah worship in Arabia. The entire fertile crescent was involved in the worship of the moon.

This, in part, explains the early success of Islam among Arab groups that traditionally had worshipped the moon god.

The use of the crescent moon as the symbol for Islam which is often placed on the top of mosques and minarets such as the ones pictured on the cover of this book, is no doubt a throwback to the days when Allah was worshipped as the moon god at the Kabah in Mecca. It is not just a symbol of the feast of Ramadan.

While this may come as a surprise to many Christians who have wrongly assumed that Allah was simply another name for the God of the Bible, educated Muslims generally understand this point.

A Muslim Taxi Driver

In one trip to Washington, D.C., I got involved in a conversation with a Muslim taxi driver from Iran.

When I asked him, "Where did Islam obtain its symbol of the crescent moon?", he responded that it was an ancient pagan symbol that was used throughout the Middle East and that it helped to convert people throughout the Middle East by adopting this pagan symbol.

When I pointed that the word Allah itself was used by the moon god cult in pre-Islamic Arabia, he agreed that this was the case.

I then pointed out that the religion and the Quran of Muhammad could be explained in terms of pre-Islamic culture, customs, and religious ideas. He agreed with this!

He went on to explain that he was a university-educated Muslim who, at this point in his life, was attempting to understand Islam from a scholarly viewpoint. As a result, he had lost his faith in Islam.

The significance of the pre-Islamic source of the name Allah cannot be overestimated.

Conclusion

In the field of comparative religions, it is understood that each of the major religions of mankind has its own peculiar concept of deity. In other words, all religions do NOT worship the same God just under different names.

The sloppy thinking that would ignore the essential differences which divide world religions is an insult to the uniqueness of world religions.

Which of the world religions holds to the Christian concept of one eternal God in three persons? When the Hindu denies the personality of God, which religions agree with this? Obviously, all men do NOT worship the same God, gods or goddesses.

The Quran's concept of deity evolved out of a pre-Islamic pagan religion. It is so uniquely Arabian that it cannot be simply reduced to Jewish or Christian beliefs. It is rooted in pagan ideas of God.

Footnotes

1. H.A.R., Gibb, Mohammedanism: An Historical Survey, (Mentor Books, N.Y., 1955), p. 38.

2. Arthur, Jeffery, ed., Islam: Muhammad and His Religion, (The Liberal Arts Press, N.Y., 1958), p.85.

3. For an interesting discussion of the origins of "allah" see: J. Blau, "Arabic Lexiographical Miscellanies," (Journal Of Semetic Studies, vol. XVII, no. 2, 1972), pgs. 173-190. That "allah" is an Arabic word is also pointed out in Hastings' Encyclopedia of Religion and Ethics, I:326.

4. Encyclopedia Of Religion and Ethics, ed. James, Hastings (T. & T. Clark, Edinburgh, 1908), I:326.

5. The Encyclopedia of Religion, ed. Paul Meagher, Thomas O'Brain, Consuela Aherne, (Corpus Pub., Washington, D.C., 1979), I:117.

6. The Encyclopedia Britannica, ibid. I:643.

7. The Encyclopedia Of Islam, ed., Houtsma, Arnold, Basset, Hartman, (E.J. Brill, Leiden, 1913), I:302

8. Encyclopedia of Islam, ed. Gibb, ibid., I:406.

9. Encyclopedia of Islam, ed. Lewis, Menage, Pellat, Schacht, (E. J. Brill, Leiden, 1971), III: 1093.

10. Encyclopedia Of Islam, ed. Lewis, Menage, Pellat, Schacht (E.J. Brill, Leiden, 1971) III:1093

11. Encyclopedia Of Religion and Ethics, ed. James Hastings, ibid., I:326.

12. Henry, Preserved Smith, The Bible and Islam: Or, The Influence Of The Old and New Testament On The Religion Of Mohammed, (Charles Scribner's Sons, N.Y., 1897) p. 102.

13. Kenneth, Cragg, The Call Of The Minaret, (Oxford University Press, N.Y., 1956), p.31.

14. William, Montgomery Watt, Muhammad's Mecca, ibid., p. vii. See also his article,"Belief In a "High God" In Pre-Islamic Mecca (Journal Of Semetic Studies, vol. 16, 1971), pgs 35-40.

15. Caesar, Farah, Islam: Beliefs And Observations, (Barrons, N.Y., 1987), p. 28.

16. E. M., Wherry, A Comprehensive Commentary On The Quran, (Otto Zeller Verlag, Osnabruck, 1973), p. 36.

17. Guillaume, Islam, ibid., p.7.

18. Encyclopedia of World Mythology and Legend, ibid., I:61.

Part Three

The God of Islam

5

Allah and the God
of the Bible

Islam claims that Allah is the same God who was revealed in the Bible. This logically implies in the positive sense that the concept of God set forth in the Quran will correspond in all points to the concept of God found in the Bible.

This also logically implies in the negative sense that if the Bible and the Quran have differing views of God, then Islam's claim is false.

This issue can only be decided by a comparison of the two documents in question. It should not be decided on the basis of religious bias on any side but by a fair reading of the text of both books.

The Attributes Of God
The Orientalist Samuel Zwemer pointed out back in 1905,

There has been a strange neglect on the part of most

writers who have described the religion of Mohammed
to study Mohammed's idea of God. It is so easy to be
misled by a name or by etymologies. Nearly all writers
take for granted that the God of the Koran is the same
being and has like attributes as Jehovah or as the Godhead
of the New Testament. Is this view correct?[1]

Most people simply assume that the God of the Bible
and the God of the Quran are one and the same God just
under different names. But, as Zwemer asked, is this
correct?

When we compare the attributes of God as found in
the Bible with the attributes of Allah found in the
Quran, it is rather obvious that these two are not the
same God.

As a matter of historical record, Christian and Muslim
scholars have been arguing over who has the true view
of God ever since Islam arose as a religion.

The biblical view of God cannot be reduced to that
of Allah any more than Allah can be reduced to the
biblical God.

The historical background concerning the origin and
meaning of the Arabian "Allah" reveals that Allah
cannot be the God of the biblical Patriarchs, the Jews,
or the Christians. Allah is merely a revamped and
magnified Arabian moon deity.

Dr. Samuel Schlorff pointed out in his article on the
essential differences between the Allah of the Quran
and the biblical God,

I believe that **the** key issue is the question of the nature
of God and how He relates to His creatures; Islam and
Christianity are, despite formal similarities, worlds apart

on that question.[2]

Let us look at some of the historic differences that have been pointed out time and again between the God of the Bible and the Allah of the Quran. These points of conflict have been noted in scholarly works for over a thousand years.[3]

These points of conflict are recognized by all standard works on the subject. Thus we will only give a brief survey of the issues involved.

Knowable vs Unknowable

1. According to the Bible, God is knowable. Jesus Christ came into this world that we might know God (John 17:3).

But in the Quran, Allah is so transcendent and exalted that no man can ever personally know him.

Thus while according to the Bible, man can come into a personal relationship with God, the Allah of the Quran is so distant, so far off, so abstract, that no one can know him.

Personal vs Non-personal

2. The God of the Bible is spoken of as a personal being with intellect, emotion and will.

This is in contrast to Allah who is not to be understood as a person. This would lower him to the level of man, according to Muslim theology.

Spiritual vs Non-spiritual

3. To the Muslim, the idea that Allah is a person or a spirit is blasphemous because this would demean the exalted One.

But that "God is a spirit" is one of the cornerstones

of the biblical nature of God (John 4:24).

Trinitarian vs Unitarian

4. The God of the Bible is one God in three persons: the Father, the Son, and the Holy Spirit. This Trinity is not three gods but one God.

When we turn to the Quran, we find that it explicitly denies the Trinity. The Quran states that God is not a Father and Jesus is not the Son of God. Neither is the Holy Spirit to be viewed as God.

Limited vs Unlimited

5. The biblical God is limited by His own immutable and unalterable nature. Thus God cannot do anything and everything.

In Titus 1:2, we are told, "God cannot lie." We are also told this in Heb. 6:18. Thus God can never act in such a way that it would contradict His divine nature (II Tim. 2:13).

But when you turn to the Quran, you discover that Allah is not limited by anything. He is not even limited by his own nature. Allah can do anything, any time, any place, anywhere with no limitations.

Trustworthy vs Capricious

6. Because the God of the Bible is limited by his own righteous nature and there are certain things He cannot do, he is completely consistent and trustworthy.

But when we turn to study the actions of Allah in the Quran, we discover that he is totally capricious and untrustworthy. He is not bound by his nature or his word.

Love Of God vs No Love Of God

7. The love of God is the chief attribute of the biblical God as revealed in such places as John 3:16. God has feelings for his creatures, especially man.

But when we turn to the Quran, we do not find the love of God presented as the chief attribute of God. Instead, the transcendence of Allah is his chief attribute.

Neither does Allah "have feelings" toward man. The love of Allah is foreign to Islamic teaching. That would reduce Allah to being a mere man- which is blasphemous to a Muslim.

Active in History vs Non-active

8. According to Islamic theology, Allah does not personally enter into human history and act as a historical agent. He always deals with the world through his word, prophets and angels. He does not personally come down and deal with man.

How different is the biblical idea of the Incarnation in which God himself enters history and acts in history to bring about man's salvation.

Attributes vs No Attributes

9. The Quran never tells us in a positive sense what God is in terms of his nature or essence. The so-called "ninety nine attributes" of Allah are all negative in form signifying what Allah is not but never telling us what he is.

The Bible gives us both positive and negative attributes for God.

Grace vs Works

10. Lastly, the Bible speaks much of the grace of

God in providing a free salvation for man through a Savior who acts as an intercessor between God and man (I Tim. 2:5).

Yet, in the Quran there is no concept of the "grace" of Allah. There is no savior or intercessor according to the Quran.

In conclusion, when you examine the attributes of the God who has revealed Himself in the Bible to the Allah who is described in the Quran, they are not one and the same God.

The Same God?

In giving this material in a lecture format, one person responded that he believed that Islam and Christianity worship the same God because "they both worship only one God."

What he failed to understand is that monotheism in and of itself does not tell us anything about the identity of the one God who is to be worshipped. In other words, it is not enough to say there is only one God if you have the wrong God.

If someone said that Ra, Isis, or Osiris was the one true God, this does not mean that Christianity and Egyptian deities are one and the same.

Someone could have taught that Baal or Molech was the one true God. Or again, the Greeks could have argued that Zeus or Jupiter was the one true living God.

But merely arguing that there is one God does not automatically mean that the one God you choose to worship happens to be the right one.

In this case, the God of the Bible has clearly revealed Himself in such a way that His nature and His names cannot be confused with the nature and names of the surrounding pagan deities.

The cult of the moon god which worshipped Allah was transformed by Muhammad into a monotheistic faith.

The obvious problem with this is that because Muhammad started with a pagan god, it is no surprise that he ended up with a pagan god.

As the German scholar Johannes Hauri pointed out,

> Mohammed's monotheism was just as much a departure from true monotheism as the polytheistic ideas . . . Mohammed's idea of God is out and out deistic.[4]

Is Allah In The Bible?

In a conversation with an Ambassador from a Muslim country, I pointed out that the name "Allah" was an Arabic word that had to do with the worship of the moon god in pre-Islamic Arabia.

As such, this Arabic word "Allah" could not be found in the Hebrew Old Testament or in the Greek New Testament.

The Ambassador used two arguments by which he hoped to prove that the Bible did speak of Allah.

First, he claimed that the name Allah was found in the biblical word "allelujah." The "alle" in the first part of the word was actually "Allah" according to him!

I pointed out to him that the Hebrew word "allelujah" is not a compound Hebrew word. That is, it is not made up of two words. It is one single Hebrew word which means "Praise to Yahweh."[5]

Also, the name of God is in the last part of the word, "jah," which has reference to Yahweh or Jehovah. The name Allah simply cannot be found in that word.

Secondly, he then proceeded to tell me that when Jesus was on the cross and he cried out, "Eli, Eli," he was actually saying "Allah, Allah."

But this is not true either. The Greek New Testament at this point gives us the Aramaic, not the Arabic, translation of a portion of Psalm 22:1. Jesus was saying, "My God, my God, why has Thou forsaken me?"

It is a far cry to go from "Eli, Eli" all the way to "Allah, Allah." It simply cannot be done.

Wrong Time Period

As a matter of historical record, it was impossible for the authors of the Bible to speak of "Allah" as God. Why?

Up until the 7th century when Muhammad made Allah into the "only" God, "Allah" was the name of an obscure pagan deity!

Since the Bible was completed long before Muhammad was ever born, how could it speak of a post-Muhammad Allah?

In reality, the name Allah never came across the lips of the authors of Scripture.

Up until the time of Muhammad, Allah was simply one pagan god among many, a particular Arabic name for the moon god as worshipped in Arabia.

The Biblical authors would have never confused Allah with Jehovah any more than they would have confused Baal with Jehovah.

Conclusion

Most uneducated Westerners assume that Allah is just another name for God. This is due to their ignorance of the differences between Allah and the God of the Bible and also due to the propaganda of Muslim evangelists who use the idea that Allah is just another name for God as an opportunity to convert Westerners to Islam.

The Bible and the Quran are two competing documents that differ in their concept of deity. This fact cannot be overlooked just because it is not in conformity to the present popularity of religious relativism.

Footnotes

1. Samuel, Zwemer, The Muslim Doctrines of God: An Essay On The Character Of Allah According To The Koran, (American Tract Society, N.Y., 1905).

2. Samuel, Schlorff, "Theological And Apologetical Dimensions Of Muslim Evangelism," (Westminster Theological Journal, vol. 42, no.2, (Spring 1980), pp. 338.

3. For the Christian view of God see: H. Spencer, Islam and The Gospel of God, (S.P.C.K., Madras, 1956) and Augustus Strong, Systematic Theology, ibid., p. 186. For the Muslim viewpoint see: Mohammad Zia Ullah, Islamic Concept of God, (Kegan Paul Inter., London, 1984).

4. Quoted in Zwemer, ibid., p. 21.

5. International Standard Bible Encyclopedia, ed. James Orr, ibid., II:1323.

Part Four

The Prophet of Islam

6

The Life of Muhammad

The life of Muhammad, with all of its interesting
twists and turns, can be known from the material that
is found in the Quran, the Hadith, and early Muslim
traditions. There are also many biographies, Muslim
and Western, which have been written concerning this
man.

Thankfully, the basic facts concerning Muhammad's life are well-known and are not issues of controversy.[1]

Birth and Early life

Muhammad was born in A.D. 570 in Mecca to
Abdullah and Aminah. He was born into the Quraysh
tribe which was in control of the city of Mecca.

The Quraysh tribe was the custodian of the Kabah
and of the religious worship centered around it.

Even though he was distantly related to the Arab
royal family of Hashim, the particular branch of the

family into which Muhammad had been born was impoverished.

Muhammad's father died before he was born and his mother died while he was still young. He was sent to live with his rich grandparents.

Muhammad's grandparents later sent him to live with a wealthy uncle who in turn later passed him on to a poor uncle who raised him the best that he could.

It is interesting to note that many of his family members never accepted Muhammad's claim to be a prophet. For example, his grandfather lived and died a pagan and never did embrace Islam.

According to the biographers and early Muslim traditions, there were no outstanding achievements accomplished by Muhammad. He was a normal Arab boy who enjoyed talking with those who travelled in the caravans. He loved to explore the desert and particularly the caves. The only thing that was unusual with his childhood was that he began to experience religious visitations.

Early Visions

According to early Muslim traditions, the young pagan Muhammad experienced miraculous visions.

There is the trustworthy account in which Muhammad claimed that a heavenly being had split open his stomach and then stirred his insides around and then sewed him back up![2]

Muhammad himself later refers to this episode in Sura 93:1 which literally translates as, "Did We not open thy breast for thee?"

While the early Muslim writers, including the relatives of Muhammad, place this in Muhammad's youth, later Muslim apologists out of embarrassment have tried to move it to a period after his call to be a prophet. But the historical evidence is entirely against this move.

As to the meaning of his belly being split open and his insides stirred, we are not told. But this story is so well documented, that it cannot be denied.

One possible explanation of these early religious episodes has to do with the fact that many Middle East scholars have felt that Muhammad was afflicted with either some kind of mental problem or the medical problem of epilepsy.

Muhammad's Mother

His mother, Aminah, was of an excitable nature and often claimed that she was visited by spirits, or jinns.

She also at times claimed to have visions and religious experiences. Thus Muhammad's mother was involved in what we call today the "occult arts" and this basic orientation seems to have been inherited by her son, Muhammad.[3]

The Possibility Of Epilepsy

But other scholars suggest that perhaps Muhammad's early visions were the result of a combination of epileptic seizures and an over active imagination.

Early Muslim tradition records the fact that when Muhammad was about to receive a "revelation" from Allah, he would often fall down on the ground, his body would begin to jerk, his eyes would roll backward, and he would perspire profusely. They would often cover him with a blanket during such episodes.

It was while Muhammad was in such a trance like

state that he would receive divine visitations. After the trance, he would arise and then proclaim what had been handed down to him.

From the description of the bodily attributes that were often connected with his trances, many scholars have stated that these were epileptic seizures.

For example, the Shorter Encyclopedia of Islam, published by Cornell University, points out that the Hadith itself describes "the half-abnormal ecstatic condition with which he was overcome." (pg. 274).

What must be remembered is that in the Arab culture of Muhammad's day, epileptic seizures were interpreted as a religious sign of either demonic possession or divine visitation.

Muhammad initially considered both options as a possible interpretation of his experience. At first he worried about the possibility that he was demon possessed. This led him to attempt to commit suicide.

But his devoted wife was able to stop him from committing suicide by persuading him that he was such a good man that he could not possibly be demon possessed. More about this later.

We are aware that to even speak of the serious possibility that Muhammad may have had epileptic seizures is very offensive to Muslims. It is blasphemous for them to even consider such an interpretation.

But we would fail to convey to the reader all the facts about Muhammad if we left this out. How can we hide from the reader what many Middle East scholars have said?

Western scholars do not deny that Muhammad had "experiences" of some kind. But they also believe that such "experiences" must be interpreted and that everyone has the right to make up his own mind as to what these experiences were.

Just as Muslims are free to interpret them as divine visitations, non-Muslims are free to interpret them as epileptic seizures, demon possession, an over active imagination, fraud, religious hysteria, or whatever else gives them an adequate explanation of what Muhammad was experiencing.[4]

The reader will have to make up his own mind. Our task is to set before him all the possible options.

In McClintock and Strong's Encyclopedia we read the following:

> Muhammad was endowed with a nervous constitution and a lively imagination. It was not at all unnatural for him to come after a time to regard himself as actually called of God to build up his people in a new faith. Muhammad, as we gather from the oldest and most trustworthy narratives, was an epileptic, and as such, was considered to be possessed of evil spirits. At first, he believed the sayings, but gradually he came to the conclusion, confirmed by his friends, that demons had no power over so pure and pious a man as he was and he conceived the idea that he was not controlled by evil spirits, but that he was visited by angels whom he, disposed to hallucinations, a vision, an audition, afflicted with the morbid state of body and mind, saw in dreams. Or even while awake, conceived he saw. What seemed to him good and true after such epileptic attacks, he esteemed revelation in which he, at least in the first stage of his pathetic course, firmly believed and which imparted to his pensive, variable character, the necessary courage and endurance all mortifications and perils.[5]

Modern Reticence

We fully understand the modern reticence to point out that Muhammad's epileptic seizures could have been the source of his religious trances.

We understand that this statement will offend the sensibilities of some Muslims. But our intent is not to offend the feelings of anyone.

Our intent is to establish that according to the descriptions of the physical characteristics which manifested themselves when Muhammad would fall into one of his trances according to early Muslim traditions, we must not automatically rule out the possibility of epilepsy.

That epileptic seizures were viewed as "visitations" of the gods or the "possession" of a person by evil spirits, is part of pre-Islamic Arabian superstition and religious life.

This reality coupled with the fact that these two options were the only ones that Muhammad himself considered as possible explanations for his trances, leads one to the conclusion that he either had epilepsy or something like it.

Western scholarship cannot simply ignore historical facts or seek to rewrite history in order to avoid hurting the feelings of those who do not want to hear the truth. Facts are facts regardless of how someone feels about them.

An entire generation of Islamic scholars have gone on record stating that we must consider the possibility that Muhammad was afflicted with epilepsy and this manifested itself early on by the vision of Muhammad's belly being split open and then later by all his "prophetic" trances.

Religious Background

As to the religious background in which Muhammad was raised, the Quraysh tribe was particularly addicted to the cult of the moon god, Allah.

They had a peculiar fondness for the three daughters of Allah, who were called Al-Lat, Al-Uzza, and Manat.

The fact that Muhammad's father was named Abdullah (lit. Abd-Allah) and his uncle Obeidullah (lit. Obeid-Allah) not only proves the pre-Islamic use of the word "Allah" but also that Muhammad's family was deeply involved in the worship of the moon god, Allah, and his three daughters.

Muhammad grew up in Mecca where the Kabah shrine had at least 360 idols and the sacred magical black stone which was considered the "good luck charm" for the Quraysh tribe.

He witnessed pilgrims coming to the Mecca every year where they would worship at the Kabah by running around it seven times, kissing the black stone, and then running down to a nearby Wady to throw stones at the devil.

It is no surprise to find that most of the elements of his religious upbringing were transferred into the religion of Islam and did not come from a "new" revelation from Allah to Muhammad.

His First Wife

His life was uneventful as a young man. At the age of 25, he was tending a caravan. The woman who owned it was 15 years older than he was and a widow. She fell in love with him and married him. Together they had two sons, though both died young, and four daughters.

One of the daughters married Uthman, who became the Caliph who later standardized the text of the Quran.

After he married the wealthy widow, Muhammad lived a life of leisure and his duties were limited to running the family produce stand in the market.

His Call To Be A Prophet

At the age of 40, Muhammad experienced once again a "visitation." As a result of his religious experience, he ultimately claimed that Allah had called him to be a prophet and an apostle.

It must be pointed out that there was no tradition of being a "prophet" or "apostle" in Arabian religion.

While the term "prophet" was used in the hope that the Jews would accept Muhammad as the next prophet, the term "apostle" was likewise used in the hope that the Christians would acknowledge him as the next apostle.

Muhammad's appeal would not only be to the pagans who already joined him in worship at the Kabah in Mecca, but also to the Jews and to the Christians.

Four Conflicting Versions

In the Quran, we are told that Allah called Muhammad to be a prophet and an apostle. But, as Dr. William Montgomery Watt observed, "Unfortunately, there are several alternative versions of these events."[6]

In other words, the Quran gives us four conflicting accounts of this original call to be a prophet. Either one of these four accounts is true and the others are false or they are all false. But they all cannot be true.

In the Quran on four different occasions,

Muhammad described his initial call to be a prophet and apostle.

We are first told in Sura 53:2-18 and Sura 81:19-24, that Allah personally appeared to Muhammad in the form of a man and that Muhammad saw and heard him.

This was later abandoned and we are then told in Sura 16:102 and Sura 26:192-194 that Muhammad's call was issued by "the Holy Spirit."

Since Muhammad does not really discuss who or what this "Holy Spirit" was, this was later abandoned.

The third account of his original call is given in Sura 15:8 where we are told that "the angels" were the ones who came down to Muhammad and announced that Allah had called him to be a prophet.

Even this account was later amended in Sura 2:97 so that it was only the angel Gabriel who issued the call to Muhammad and handed down the Quran to him.

This last account of his original call was influenced by the fact that Gabriel had played a significant role in the birth both of Jesus and John the Baptist.

Some scholars believe that Muhammad assumed that it was only appropriate that the next great prophet in line, being himself, should also be issued the call by Gabriel.

This fourth and last account of his initial call is the one that most Muslims and non-Muslims have heard.

But we must point out that the same "incident" had four conflicting accounts given of it in the Quran.

Islamic Revelation

We should point out, at this point, that the concept of revelation in Islamic thought is not the same as held by Christians concerning the Bible.

The word "revelation" in Arabic literally means "handed down." It means that the Quran did not come "through" or "by" any man, Muhammad included. The Quran only came "to" man, in this case, Muhammad.

Thus there are no human authors of the Quran. Allah speaks directly to man and man is the receiver and not the originator of the Quran.

This is in contrast to the biblical authors who even identified themselves as the ones who wrote their particular books.

Thus Christians have no difficulty in saying Isaiah wrote Isaiah or Matthew wrote Matthew. They do not feel that this lessens or limits the inspiration of the Bible in any way.

But with the Quran there is the denial that there is any human or earthly sources for the material that was "handed down" from heaven by Allah through Gabriel.

Doubts and Suicide

After this initial religious experience in which he felt that he had been called to a prophet and an apostle, Muhammad began to have grave doubts about his sanity. In particular, he was frightened that he was demon possessed.

The bodily characteristics connected with his trances seemed, even to Muhammad, to parallel those in his community who would fall down in fits. It was believed that they were possessed by devils.

He became so depressed that he decided to commit suicide. But on his way to the place where he was going to kill himself, he fell once again into a seizure.

He experienced another vision in which he felt that he had been told not to kill himself but that he was truly called of God.

Yet, even after this religious experience, he still became depressed and filled with doubt.

He Begins His Preaching

When he finally opened his heart to his wife, she supported him in that she felt that God had indeed called him to be a prophet and an apostle. She encouraged him to begin to share this good news with their family and friends.

Muhammad at first shared his call only with his family and friends in secret. Indeed, his first converts were members of his own family.

Opposition Begins

But soon after his message became public, he was subject to abuse and ridicule by the population at large and even by members of his own family.

At one point, the hostility against Muhammad was such that people in Mecca had laid siege to the section of the city where Muhammad lived and he faced a very difficult situation.

The Satanic Verses

In order to appease his pagan family members and the members of the Quraysh tribe, he decided that the best thing he could do was to admit that it was perfectly proper to pray to and to worship the three daughters of Allah — Al-Lat, Al-Uzza, and Manat.

This led to the famous "satanic verses" in which Muhammad, in a moment of weakness and supposedly under the inspiration of Satan, according to Muslim authorities, succumbed to the temptation to appease the pagan mobs in Mecca. (Sura 53:19)

The literature on the "satanic verses" is so vast that an entire volume could be written just on this one issue. Every general and Islamic reference work, Muslim or Western, deals with it as well as all the biographies of Muhammad.

The story of Muhammad's temporary appeasement of the pagans by allowing them their polytheism cannot be ignored or denied. It is a fact that is supported by all scholars, Western and Muslim.

We are aware that there are a few modern Muslim apologists who reject the story of the "satanic verses." But we must point out that they do so not on the basis of any historical or textual evidence. Their objection is based solely on the grounds that Muhammad was sinless and therefore could not have done this![7] Since this is circular reasoning, it deserves no further comment.

Muhammad Gets Rebuked

When his disciples at Medina heard of Muhammad's "fall" into polytheism, they rushed to him with rebukes and counsel.

Muhammad would later claim that Gabriel himself had come down from heaven and rebuked him for allowing Satan to inspire him to concede to the Meccan worship of the daughters of Allah.

He then reverted back to his monotheism and stated that Allah can "abrogate," i.e. take away verses in the Quran if he deems fit. He then removed the "satanic verses" from the Quran and once again condemned the worship of the three daughters of Allah.[8]

This, of course, led to no end of ridicule. The pagan Meccans with glee pointed out that Muhammad's Allah simply could not make up his mind.

At one point, Muhammad claimed that Allah said they may not worship the three daughters of Allah. Then Allah said that they may worship the three daughters. And now, once again, they are being told that they may not worship the three daughters. Cannot Allah make up his mind?

Forced To Flee

Because of the ridicule and the hostility that was now growing, he left Mecca and went to Ta-if.

Finding no success or converts in Ta-if, he decided to return to Mecca.

On his way back to Mecca, according to the Quran in Sura 46:29-35; 72:1-28, Muhammad preached to and converted the jinn, or the genies!

According to the Quran, the jinns in turn preached Islam to the people. Thus, the male and female spirits who inhabited the trees, the rocks, and the waters of Arabia were now Muslims and under the control of Muhammad.[9]

This is a classic form of shamanism in which Muhammad could now claim to be in control of the spirits of the earth.

Once back in Mecca, he found that the hostility to his message had grown. The merchants were particularly deeply concerned lest the financial base of the city be destroyed by his attack on the worship of the idols that were placed at the Kabah.

Flight To Medina

Muhammad once again left Mecca and this time moved to Medina where his preaching was received.

While at Medina, Muhammad realized that his family and tribe would not give up their worship of idols unless they were forced by physical violence to do so.

The First Battle

He began to test his own power in making war by first sending out six followers who attacked a caravan, killed a man, enslaved others, and looted the caravan. This is the Nakhla Raid.

All of this took place during the month which traditionally, in Arab times, was the month of truce and peace.

Muhammad received no end of criticism for violating a time of truce observed by the entire community in order to loot the caravan.[10]

The Second Battle

Now that the taste of loot and blood was in the mouth of his disciples, Muhammad led the second battle himself and his followers won the battle of Badr.

This great success led to more followers who wanted to get in on the fighting, killing, and looting.

Muhammad Turns On The Jews

It was at this time that Muhammad decided that the Jews were not going to convert. The Muslim scholar Ali Dashti comments,

After the Nakhla raid, further attacks on Qorayshite

caravans and unfriendly tribes met with success and helped to make the financial position of the Moslems more secure. This raiding opened the way for the acquisition of power by the Prophet Mohammad and his companions and for their eventual domination of all Arabia; but the immediate step which secured the economic base and strengthened the prestige of the Moslems was their seizure of the property of the Jews of Yathreb.[11]

Muhammad at first tried to encourage the Jews to accept his prophethood by preaching monotheism, observing the Jewish Sabbath, praying toward Jerusalem, appealing to Abraham and the patriarchs, adopting some of their dietary laws and by praising their Scriptures.

But now it was obvious the wealthy Jewish merchants were not coming over to become his disciples. So Muhammad decided to drop the observance of Jewish rites.

He changed the direction of prayer from Jerusalem to Mecca, dropped the Saturday Sabbath and adopted a Friday Sabbath instead. He once again adopted the pagan religious rites in which he had been raised by his family.

But this was not all. It was at this time that Muhammad began killing Jews. At first he would send out assassins to kill individual Jews and then later on he would attack Jewish settlements.

There was a financial reason as well as a religious one for his attacks on the Jews. Some of the Jewish settlements were centers of the gold and silver trade and by conquering such places, great wealth could be obtained quickly.

The Encyclopedia Britannica points out,

When he discovered their military incompetence he appears to have been unable to resist the temptation to appropriate their goods; and his attack on the flourishing Jewish settlement of Khaibar appears to have been designed to satisfy his discontented adherents by an accession of plunder.[12]

His First Defeat

The Meccans had decided that Muhammad was a true threat and approached with a large army headed by Uhud.

Muhammad lost this battle although he had predicted victory. He was struck in the mouth by a sword, lost several teeth, and almost died. It was a terrible defeat for him and his followers.

Some of his followers fell away as they felt they had been deceived. They had gone forth in battle expecting a glorious victory and much loot but, instead, they had to retreat in defeat with their leader and so-called prophet who was severely wounded!

Why the Meccans did not follow through and destroy Muhammad and his forces is not known.

But after inflicting sufficient casualties to appease the sense of Arab vengeance, the Meccans returned to their towns and left Muhammad in peace.

The Jewish Settlements

Muhammad then turned his attention once again to the Jews again who were easier targets than the Meccans.

He began killing and looting Jewish settlements. In one Jewish town, after they had surrendered, from 700 to 1,000 men were beheaded in one day while all the women and children were sold into slavery and the possessions of the town were looted! This fact is supported by Muslim scholars as well as by Western historians.[13]

Final Triumph Over Mecca

Muhammad then turned his attention once again to Mecca. His forces had grown sufficiently so that he now had a large army in the field.

A treaty was established with the authorities of Mecca in which peace between Muhammad and Mecca was to last for ten years.

On the basis of the promise of peace, Muhammad and his followers would be allowed to make the pilgrimage to the Kabah and Mecca. He would be free to seek to persuade people by moral persuasion and preaching to adopt Islam, but he was not to use force.

Within a year, Muhammad broke the treaty and with an army of thousands of followers, forced Mecca to surrender to his leadership.

Muhammad then became the undisputed political tyrant of Mecca as well as its undisputed religious head.

He cleansed the temple at Kabah of all its idols. He suppressed all idol worship by violence. Some of the people he had killed were ones with whom he had a personal vendetta.

For example, there was a woman poetess who had ridiculed him and had pointed out that some of the material in the Quran had actually been stolen from her poet father. She was put to death in order to silence her.

Muhammad had now achieved unbelievable success. As the undisputed head and potentate of Mecca

and of its religious center, Arab tribesmen began to
flock to him from all sides.

Muhammad's Personal Life

In terms of his personal life, Muhammad had two
great weaknesses. The first was that of greed. By
looting caravans and Jewish settlements he had amassed
fabulous wealth for himself, his family, and his tribe.

Secondly, his next greatest weakness was women.
Although in the Quran he would limit his followers to
having four wives, he himself took more than four
wives and concubines.

The question of the number of women with whom
Muhammad was sexually involved either as wives,
concubines or devotees was made a point of contention
by the Jews in Muhammad's day. Ali Dashti comments,

> All the commentaries agree that verse 57 of sura 4 (on-
> Nesa) was sent down after the Jews criticized Mohammad's
> appetite for women, alleging that he had nothing to do
> except to take wives.[14]

Since polygamy was practiced in the Old Testament
by such Patriarchs as Abraham, the mere fact that
Muhammad had more than one wife is not sufficient in
and of itself to discount his claim to prophethood.

This does not negate the fact that the issue has historical merit in terms of trying to understand Muhammad as a man.

But it also poses a tremendous logical problem for
Muslims. The Quran in Sura 4:3 forbids the taking of
more than four wives. To take any more would be

sinful.

One Muslim apologist with whom I was conversing used circular reasoning at this point. His argument was as follows:

> Muhammad was sinless. The Quran makes taking more than four wives a sin. Therefore Muhammad could not have taken more than four wives. Why? Because Muhammad was sinless.

I pointed out that the question of how many wives Muhammad or anyone else had should be answered on the basis of the historical and literary evidence and not blind faith.

Thankfully, not all Muslims "row with only one oar in the water" by using circular reasoning.

The Muslim scholar and statesman, Ali Dashti, gives the following list of the women in Muhammad's life.

The Women In Muhammad's Harem
1. Khadija
2. Sawda
3. Aesha
4. Omm Salama
5. Hafsa
6. Zaynab (of Jahsh)
7. Jowayriya
8. Omm Habiba
9. Safiya
10. Maymuna (of Hareth)

11. Fatema
12. Hend
13. Asma (of Saba)
14. Zaynab (of Khozayma)
15. Habla
16. Asma (of Noman)
17. Mary (the Christian)
18. Rayhana
19. Omm Sharik
20. Maymuna (not of Hareth)
21. Zaynab (a 3rd one)
22. Khawla

Several observations need to be given about the above list.

First, the first 16 women were wives.

Second, numbers 17 and 18 were slaves or concubines.

Third, the last four women were neither wives or slaves but devout Muslim women who "gave" themselves to satisfy Muhammad's sexual desires.

Fourth, Zaynab of Jahsh was originally Muhammad's adopted son's wife. The fact that Muhammad took her for himself has been problematic to many people, Muslims included.

Fifth, Aesha was only eight or nine years old when Muhammad took her to his bed. This facet of Muhammad's sexual appetite is particularly distressing to Westerners.

While in Islamic countries an eight or nine year old girl can be given in marriage to an adult male, in the West, most people would shudder to think of an eight or nine year old little girl being given in marriage to anyone.

This aspect of Muhammad's personal life is something that many scholars pass over once again because they do not want to hurt the feelings of Muslims.

Yet, history cannot be rewritten to avoid confronting the facts that Muhammad had unnatural desires for little girls.

Sixth, Mary, the Coptic Christian, refused to marry Muhammad because she would not renounce Christianity and embraced Islam. She bravely chose to remain a slave rather than convert.

The documentation for all the women in Muhammad's harem is so vast and has been presented so many times by able scholars that only those who use circular reasoning can object to it.

Muhammad's Death

As to the circumstances of Muhammad's death in the year A. D. 632, there is some confusion.

The traditional view is that his death was due to poisoning by a Jewish woman whose relatives were murdered in one of Muhammad's pogroms against the Jews.

Yet, because this poisoning incident may have taken place one to two years before his death, it seems hard to believe that the poison did not kill him until that time.

It is also true from the early biographers that Muhammad had no premonition of his own death.

Thus he had made no arrangements for a successor. He had not set up any kind of governmental bureaucracy to run things in event of his death.

Neither had he gathered or put together his various

revelations into what is now known as the Quran. His death was sudden and gave him no time whatsoever to arrange his own affairs.

This is why Islam was soon to break apart into warring sects such as the Shiites versus the Sunis. Chaos followed because Muhammad had not clearly spelled out what was to be done after his death.

Conclusion

The amazing genius and forceful personality of Muhammad enabled him to take a minor pagan cult of the worship of the moon god Allah and turn it into the second largest religion in the world!

Footnotes

1. Dozens of such biographies, Muslim and Western, are listed in the bibliography.

2. Alfred, Guillaume, Islam, ibid., pgs. 24-25.

3. John, McClintock and James, Strong, Cyclopedia of Biblical, Theological, and Ecclesiastical Literature, (Baker Book House, Grand Rapids, 1981 reprint) 6:406.

4. Hurgronji, Mohammedanism, (Hyperion Press, Westport, Conn., 1981), p.46.

5. McClintock and Strong, ibid., 6:406.

6. For a full treatment of this contradiction see: W. Montgomery Watt, Muhammad's Mecca, ibid., pgs. 54-68

7. For a Muslim apologetical work aimed at overturning nearly every point raised by Western scholarship, see Muhammad Husayn Haykal's book, The Life Of Muhammad, (Crescent Pub., Delhi, 1976). His book is marred by the constant use of circular reasoning and by an utter lack of any scholarship. For detailed discussions by Western scholars see Guillaume, Watt, Gibb, Jeffery, etc.

8. W. Montgomery Watt, ibid., pgs. 70-72, 86-93.

9. See Guillaume, ibid., pgs 37-38.

10. Ali Dashti, ibid., p. 86.

11. Ali Dashti, ibid., p. 87.

12. Encyclopedia Britannica, ibid., 15:648.

13. For Muslim documentation, see Ali Dashti, ibid., pgs. 88-91. For Western scholars, see: Alfred Guillaume, Islam, ibid., pgs. 47-48.

14. Dashti, ibid., pgs. 120-138

7

Muhammad and Jesus Christ

Islam claims that Muhammad and Jesus of Nazareth were both Muslims and both prophets sent by Allah. Thus these two mighty prophets must coincide in all points and never contradict each other.

After all, if the same Allah sent both of them, it is only logical to assume that their ministries and messages cannot in principle contradict each other. Otherwise, Allah would be contradicting himself!

This is, of course, received as a tenet of faith by the orthodox Muslims and is not open to question in their minds.

Yet, Western scholars cannot gratuitously accept such a belief without first comparing the ministries and messages of these men to see if in fact they are in complete accord.

How To Do It

But how is this to be done? Everyone agrees that the life and teaching of Muhammad can be reconstructed from the Quran. But what about Jesus of Nazareth?

Some Muslims attempt to block any attempt to compare the biblical Jesus to the quranic Muhammad by claiming that the Bible is hopelessly corrupt and that the Jesus of the New Testament is not the true Jesus. Thus no comparison can be made.

But this approach lands them in yet deeper problems. Since the Quran uses these same Gospels for its information on Jesus such as his virgin birth, if they are corrupt, then so is the Quran.

The modern Muslim attempt to limit our informaton about Jesus to what the Quran says about him is once again circular reasoning.

In one friendly "debate" with a Muslim student, the following conversation took place.

Muslim: The Quran is true in all things.

Non-Muslim: But it contradicts the biblical Jesus.

Muslim: Then the Bible is corrupt.

Non-Muslim: But how do you know that the Bible is "corrupt?" Do you have any textual proof?

Muslim: I don't need any textual proof because I know that the Bible is corrupt.

Non-Muslim: But how do you know this?

Muslim: The Quran is true in all things.

A Different Approach

Perhaps the best way to deal with this is to lay aside all a priori assumptions of the inspiration of either the Bible or the Quran and simply compare the Bible and the Quran as two literary documents.

This literary approach will keep us objective in comparing Jesus and Muhammad. In this way the supposed inspiration of either book does not logically have any bearing on the literary issue.

It would thus be highly instructive if we compare the life of Muhammad to the life of Jesus Christ.

Founding Documents Only

In this literary comparison, we will restrict ourselves to the founding literary documents of each religion.

The life of Muhammad will be drawn only from the Quran just as the life of Jesus will be drawn only from the New Testament. This will keep things honest and fair.

We will not utilize any of the later Muslim legends which tried desperately to elevate Muhammad's life above mediocrity and to add to it elements of the miraculous.

Due to limitations of space in this book, we can only give a brief survey of some of the ways that Muhammad and Jesus can be compared.

Those readers who wish to study this issue in depth should consult Alfred Guillaume's book, The Traditions of Islam, which is the fullest treatment we know of on the subject.

Prophecy

First, the birth, life, death, and resurrection of Jesus were clearly prophesied in the Old Testament.

Several examples will suffice: Micah 5:2 gives us the very name of the town in which the Messiah would be born. On the day Christ died, no less than 33 Old Testament prophecies were fulfilled. The coming of Christ was preceded by the preaching of John the Baptist, in the spirit and power of Elijah, according to the prophecy in Isa. 40 and Malachi 4.

This is in stark contrast to the coming of Muhammad whose coming was not predicted by pagan soothsayers, Old Testament prophets, or New Testament apostles.

That this point is well taken is proven by the extreme lengths some Muslims will go to manufacture some biblical prophecies for the coming of Muhammad. Some of these claims are so outlandish that they only need be noted to refute them.

For example, one American black Muslim tried to convince me that the word "Amen" in the Bible actually meant "Ahmend" i.e., Muhammad!

The vain attempt of some modern Muslims to claim that when Jesus predicted the coming of a comforter in John chapters 14, 15 and 16, that this had reference to Muhammad, falls to the ground when one reads John 14:26 where the comforter is specifically identified as the Holy Spirit whom the Father will send in the name of Jesus Christ.

Other biblical passages have been cited by Muslim apologists from time to time but without any concern for the original language or the context of the text. They have been ably dealt with by Western scholars.[1]

Muhammad never claimed to be the Holy Spirit who had come in the name of Jesus Christ. Thus we find that while the coming of Christ was preceded by numerous prophecies, the coming of Muhammad was not predicted by anyone.

Births

Second, the birth of Jesus Christ was miraculous in that he was conceived by the Holy Spirit in the womb of the Virgin Mary.

The Quran and orthodox Islam fully accept the virgin birth of Jesus. It is only in modern times that we find some small heretical Muslim groups who deny and ridicule the doctrine of the virgin birth of Jesus.

They do this out of a reaction to the fact that there was nothing miraculous or supernatural about the birth of Muhammad. He was the natural product of the sexual union of his father and mother.

Sinlessness

Third, according to the New Testament, Jesus Christ lived a perfect and sinless life (II Cor. 5:21).

When his enemies came to accuse Jesus before Pilate or Herod, they had to invent charges because no one could find anything against him.

But when we turn to the life of Muhammad, we find that he was a normal human being engaged in the same sins which afflict all of us. He lied; he cheated; he lusted; he failed to keep his word, etc. He was neither perfect nor sinless.

Indeed, in Sura 18:110, Muhammad is commanded by Allah, "Say, I am but a man like yourselves."

Those Muslims who claim that Muhammad was sinless just like Jesus have failed to note Sura 40:55, where Allah told Muhammad to repent of his sins!

Mohammed Pickthall translates this passage as, "Ask forgiveness of thy sin."

The only way out of this passage is to state that Allah was wrong to ask Muhammad to ask for forgiveness because he had nothing to forgive! [2]

Miracles

Fourth, during his lifetime, Jesus did many great and mighty miracles. He healed the sick, raised the dead, cast out demons, and even ruled the wind and the waves.

But according to the Quran in dozens of places such as Sura 17:91-95, Muhammad never performed a single miracle.

The only sign that Muhammad would point to was the existence of his revelations, the Suras, that made up the Quran. (Sura 29:47-51)

Prof. Alfred Guillaume pointed out,

Controversy with Christians on the rival merits of Jesus and Muhammad may fairly be regarded as the origin of the pretended miracles, flatly contradicting the plain statement of the great Arabian and those of many of his immediate followers that he was not sent with power to work miracles. Whether the object of the inventors was to elevate their prophet to a position equal to that held by Jesus in the estimation of His servants, or whether it was to furnish themselves and their pupils with a messenger of God who satisfied a natural craving of the human heart for a visible manifestation of divine power it is not our purpose to determine. There are good reasons for believing that deliberate imitation was resorted to for the reasons already given, and because the ashabu-l-hadith did not stop at ascribing the works of Christ to their prophet. His words and those of his apostles are freely drawn on and put into the mouth of Muhammad.[3]

Thus Muhammad did no miracles. He did not heal the sick, raise the dead, cast out demons, or rule the wind and the waves. He had no more power than any normal man.

Ali Dashti comments,

Moslems, as well as others, have disregarded the historical facts. They have continually striven to turn this man [Muhammad] into an imaginary superhuman being, a sort of God in human clothes, and have generally ignored the ample evidence of his humanity. They have been ready . . . to present these fantasies as miracles.[4]

Many Iranians have been raised on a diet of myth and are ready to believe that any emamzada, of however ancestry, can at any moment perform a miracle. But if they were to read the Qoron, they would be surprised to find no report of a miracle in it at all. They would learn from twenty or more Qoronic passages that whenever the Prophet Mohammad was asked by doubters to perform a miracle, he either stayed silent or said that he would not do so because he was a human being like any other, with no function except to communicate, to be a "bringer of good news and a warner."[5]

The Love Of God

Fifth, according to the New Testament, Jesus preached the love of God. He was the greatest example of God's love in that,

For God so loved the world that He gave His only Son that whoever believed in Him should not perish but have everlasting life. (John 3:16)

In contrast, we do not have any record in the Quran of Muhammad ever preaching the love of God.

As a matter of fact, God's love for man or man's love for God do not play any significant role in the preaching of Muhammad, the Quran or the religion of Islam.

Whereas Christianity can point to the coming of Christ as the greatest proof and example that God loves mankind, Islam cannot point to anything that reveals the love of God.

Human and Divine Nature

Six, according to the New Testament, Jesus Christ was unique in that he was divine as well as human. This is why Jesus is called "God" in John 1:1,18; 20:28; Acts 20:28; Rom. 5:9; Tit. 2:13; II Pet. 2:1, etc.

When we turn to Muhammad, we find that he was only a man.

On Beauty Of Speech

Seven, when you study the speeches of Jesus as given in the Gospels, for example the Sermon on the Mount, you find that Jesus was the greatest speaker who ever lived. Even His enemies had to confess that no man ever spoke as He spoke.

But when you turn to the ecstatic confused speeches of Muhammad as found in the Quran, you do not find anything outstanding. There is nothing which matches the beauty, substance, or style of the way that Jesus preached the gospel during His lifetime.

A High Moral Example

Eight, the way Jesus lived and the way He was willing to die for sinners, has given us a high moral example to follow.

But when you turn to the example of Muhammad, you do not find a high moral example. You find him involved in many acts which must be deemed as immoral and unjust.

Killing Or Robbing

Nine, Jesus never killed or robbed anyone. If He had done so, this surely would have been brought up during His trial.

When we turn and look at the life of Muhammad we find that he clearly killed and robbed people in the name of Allah according to the Quran.

Coercion

Ten, Jesus never used physical violence to force people to believe His message or to accept Him as the Messiah.

As a matter of fact, when Peter took out his sword, Jesus told him to put it back in its sheath, because physical persuasion through violence was not the way of his kingdom. (Matt. 26:51-54)

But when we turn to the example of Muhammad, we find that he frequently used physical violence to force people to give up their idols and to accept Islam.

Directing Disciples To Kill

Eleven, Jesus never instructed His followers by way of command, example, or precept to kill in His name, to rob in His name, or to subdue enemies in His name.

But Muhammad did. He taught his disciples by example, command, and precept that they could and should kill and rob in Allah's name and force people to submit to Islam.

On Taking Another Man's Wife

Twelve, Jesus did not take any man's wife.

But Muhammad did. He even took the wife of his adopted son to be his own wife.

Child Brides

Thirteen, Jesus could not be described as a child molester or someone who was sexually involved with young children.

But this is the only description that one can give of Muhammad's marriage to an eight year old little girl who was still playing with her dolls according to the Hadith.

Unclean Foods

Fourteen, Jesus relinquished Jewish dietary laws for His followers and made all foods clean (Mark 7:14-23).

Muhammad, on the other hand, maintained the dietary laws which were in usage in his day and thus his followers are forbidden to eat pork or drink wine.

On Dying For Others

Fifteen, when Jesus Christ died, he died for the sins of his people in order to deliver them from the wrath of God (I Cor. 15:3-4).

But when Muhammad died, he died for his own sins. He did not die for anyone.

Resurrection

Sixteen, Jesus did not remain dead but he conquered sin, Hell and the grave and rose again on the third day bodily and physically in the same body that had hung on the cross. Just as He died for our sins, he arose again according to the Scriptures for our justification.

But when Muhammad died, he stayed dead. He did not rise from the dead. Muhammad is dead while Jesus Christ is alive.

Ascension

Seventeen, Jesus ascended bodily into Heaven. This was witnessed by the disciples in Acts 1:9-11.

But Muhammad did not ascend into Heaven. The Quran never states that he ascended.

Heavenly Intercession

Eighteen, Jesus is now in Heaven as our intercessor and Saviour, the only mediator between God and man.

But Muhammad is not an intercessor or a saviour. As a matter of fact, the Quran states that there is no intercessor or saviour (Sura 6:51, 70;10:3, etc.). You have to save yourself.

Worship

Nineteen, in the New Testament, Jesus was worshipped as a living Saviour (John 20:28).

But the Quran never speaks of so worshipping Muhammad. That would be blasphemous.

Muslims will admit that Muhammad should not be worshipped by anyone because he was only a man.

Personal Relationship

Twenty, according to the New Testament, man can have a personal relationship with Jesus Christ as He enters into their heart through His Spirit at conversion. This is why Christians talk about their love of Jesus.

On the other hand, what Muslim speaks of Muhammad in terms of loving him? There is no personal relationship possible with Muhammad. He is dead!

Returning To Earth

Twenty-one, Jesus will return to resurrect and judge all men. Even orthodox Muslims will often admit that this is clearly true.

But, at the same time, it must be stated that there is

no teaching in the Quran that says that Muhammad will return one day or that he will resurrect or judge anyone.

In Search Of The Historical Muhammad

Now to be sure, Western scholars are perfectly aware of the fact that in later conflicts between Muslims and Christians there were those Muslims who attempted to renovate the life of Muhammad so that it would more closely correspond to the life of Jesus Christ.

According to Ali Dashti, these stories are, "an example of myth-making and history-fabrication of Moslems."[6]

These later legends which speak of predictions of Muhammad's coming, a supernatural element to that birth, miracles, a sinless and perfect life for Muhammad, and ascension even into Heaven, etc. are clearly not part of the Quran or early Muslim teaching.

As all the standard reference works point out, they are later fabrications made by embarrassed Muslims who were faced with the rather obvious fact that Muhammad was inferior to Jesus Christ.

This led them to remold the life of Muhammad to parallel the life and miracles of Jesus. As Prof. Guillaume points out,

> Muslim theologians . . . borrowed also events from the life of Jesus, attributing them to their prophet.[7]

> Muhammadan apologists could not afford to allow their apostle to labour under the disadvantage apparent when his everyday mundane life was compared with the mighty works of Christ . . . the curious and interesting fact is that

that the later picture of Muhammad approximates in tradition ever closely to that of the Jesus of the Gospels.[8]

A Hindu Parallel

We are reminded of the followers of Krishna in India who, in response to the Christian teaching that Jesus died on the cross for our sins, immediately answered, "Well, then Krishna too must have died on a cross for our sins."

This fabrication did not last long as it was revealed that in all the literary sources concerning Krishna, no such death or crucifixion was mentioned until AFTER the followers of Krishna had engaged in debate with Christians.

In the same way, Muslim legendary material concerning the miracles of Muhammad all date AFTER heated polemical debates between Christians and Muslims.

These myths and legends were created in response to the challenge that Jesus Christ was obviously superior to Muhammad.

Conclusion

To any rational mind who examines the differences between the biblical Jesus and the quranic Muhammad, it is obvious that Jesus and Muhammad did not both come from the same God. They did not live or preach like each other. On all the essential issues they were poles apart.

Footnotes

1. Muslims have cited such passages as Gen. 49:10; Deut. 18:15-18; 32:21 33:2; Psalm 45; 149; Isa. 21:7; 432:1-4, 10-12, etc.. For the most detailed Western response to these claims, see: C. Pfander, Balance of Truth, (The Religious Tract Society, London, 1910) pgs. 228f, 252f. John Gilchrist, Is Muhammed Foretold In The Bible?, (Jesus To The Muslims, Benoni, South Africa, 1987). See also the article by Percy Smith, "Did Jesus Foretell Ahmed?" (Muslim World, vol. 12, (1922), pgs. 71f;

2. Alfred, Guillaume, The Traditions of Islam, (The Clarendon Press, London, 1924) pgs. 132-149

3. Guillaume, Traditions, ibid., p. 138.

4. Ali, Dashti, ibid., p. 1.

5. ibid., p. 38.

6. ibid., p. 3.

7. Guillaume, Traditions, ibid., pg. 133.

8. ibid., pgs. 134-135.

Part Five

The Sacred Book of Islam

8

The Structure of the Quran

When anyone who is familiar with the Bible picks up a Quran and begins to read it through, there is the immediate recognition that he is dealing with an entirely different kind of literature than what he finds in the Bible.

Whereas the Bible contains much historical narrative, the Quran contains very little. Whereas the Bible goes out of its way to explain unfamiliar terminology or territory, the Quran does not.

Structural Differences

In fact, the very way that the Bible is structured, being a library of 66 books, reveals that it is ordered according to chronology, subject and theme.

But when you turn to the Quran, you find a jumbled and confused ordering of individual Suras.

Some Western scholars have stated that the structure of the Quran is so mixed up, jumbled and confused that it requires the utmost sense of duty for anyone to plow through it!

Western Comments

The Scottish scholar Thomas Carlyle said,

> It is a toilsome reading as I ever undertook, a wearisome, confused jumble, crude, incondite. Nothing but a sense of duty could carry any European through the Koran.[1]

The German scholar Salomon Reinach stated,

> From the literary point of view, the Koran has little merit. Declamation, repetition, puerility, a lack of logic and coherence strike the unprepared reader at every turn. It is humiliating to the human intellect to think that this mediocre literature has been the subject of innumerable commentaries, and that millions of men are still wasting time in absorbing it.[2]

Even the historian Edward Gibbon, who along with Reinach can hardly be accused of being Christians, described the Quran as,

> An incoherent rhapsody of fable, and precept, and declamation, which sometimes crawls in the dust, and sometimes is lost in the clouds.[3]

McClintock and Strong's encyclopedia concludes that,

> The matter of the Koran is exceedingly incoherent and sententious, the book evidently being without any logical

order of thought either as a whole or in its parts. This agrees with the desultory and incidental manner in which it is said to have been delivered.[4]

Even the Muslim scholar Dashti laments the literary defects of the Quran.

Unfortunately the Qor'an was badly edited and its contents are very obtusely arranged. All students of the Qor'an wonder why the editors did not use the natural and logical method of ordering by date of revelation, as in 'Ali b. Taleb's lost copy of the text.

The standard Islamic reference work, The Concise Encyclopedia of Islam, refers to the "disjointed and irregular character" of the text of the Quran.[6]

The Titles Of The Quran
The titles of various Suras often seem unfamiliar to Western ears. For example,

Sura 2 The Cow
Sura 7 Spoils
Sura 16 The Bee
Sura 18 The Cave

Pre-Islamic Arabian Parallels
To find literary parallels to the Quran, one must search into the pre-Islamic Arabic literature where we find numerous examples of such ecstatic and often confused poetic material.

Mecca and Medina
Muhammad's religious ministry was spread over

two different periods. The first one took place in Mecca beginning at least by the year 612 A.D. and lasted around ten years.

The other period is centered in Medina and once again it lasted around ten years until Muhammad's death in 632 A.D.

This two-fold basic division of Meccan ministry and Medinan ministry has been acknowledged by most scholars in the field.

An Unforeseen Death

As we have already pointed out, Muhammad had not foreseen his own death although he had claimed to be a prophet of God. Thus Muhammad had made no preparations for the gathering together of his revelations so that they could be placed into one document.

No Original Manuscripts

From historical accounts that are unimpeachably accurate and trustworthy, we know that whenever Muhammad fell into one of his seizures or trances and then spoke to others, he did not write these things down on a manuscript.

Despite the farfetched claims of some modern Muslim apologists, Muhammad himself did not write or prepare the final manuscript of the Quran.

His death was unexpected, not only by his followers, but also by him. He did not even have the opportunity to gather together the scattered records of some of his Suras.

Bones, Leaves and Stones

It was left to Muhammad's followers to try to write down what he said. These records were written on whatever was handy when Muhammad fell into one of his unpredictable trances.

The Concise Encyclopedia of Islam comments,

> The Koran was collected from the chance surfaces on which it had been inscribed: "from pieces of papyrus, flat stones, palm leaves, shoulder blades and ribs of animals, pieces of leather, wooden boards, and the hearts of men.[7]

Trustworthy accounts reveal that those who heard Muhammad would write down what he said on the leg or thigh bone of dead animals, palm leaves and mats, stones, the bark of trees, etc.

Even the internationally known Muslim scholar Abdul Mandudi admits that the Quran was originally "recorded on leaves of date-palms, barks of trees, bones, etc."[8]

The strange materials on which the Quran was written is verified by all general reference works such as the encyclopedias and by the standard reference works on Islam.

When there was nothing around which could be written on, the attempt was made to memorize it as closely as possible.

According to Mandudi, the task that confronted the followers of Muhammad after his unexpected demise was to gather together the scattered sermons of Muhammad, some of which were written on biodegradable articles such as tree bark, and others which were not written down but committed only to memory.[9]

This, of course, created great difficulty. Some of the tree bark crumbled and broke and some of the stones were lost.

Worse yet, the Muslim statesman Ali Dashti noted that animals at times ate the palm leaves or mats on which the Suras had been recorded![10]

Some of those who were the only ones who remembered certain Suras died in battle before they had the opportunity to commit to writing what they had heard.

The gathering together of Quranic material lasted for several years. Much confusion reigned as the memory of one person would not exactly correspond to the memory of another.

This is a sad fact of human nature that cannot be overlooked. When more than one person is present and hears the same speech, there can often arise a disagreement as to exactly what was said.

As we shall see later on, this was overcome by the use of physical force and the attempt to coerce people to use one particular version of what Muhammad said as opposed to other versions.

The Order Of The Suras

As you pick up the Quran, you will discover that the 114 Suras, or revelations, given to Muhammad are not laid out in the chronological order in which Muhammad received them.

If this were so, then the first Sura would be the first revelation Muhammad received and the last Sura would be the last revelation.

Neither is the Quran laid out in terms of a progressive historical narrative in which we follow the life, actions, and teachings of Muhammad from beginning to end.

We are confronted instead with a jumbled mass of

Suras which defy any natural organization according
to chronology or logic.

The way that the Quran was put together by those left
behind after Muhammad died was to do so on the basis
of size. Thus the Quran is arranged from the biggest
Sura down to the smallest Sura irrespective of the chronology in which an individual Sura was given.

Mass Confusion

This causes tremendous problems and confusion. In
the Quran one will often find that what is clearly
commanded in the first part of the Quran is "abro-
gated," i.e., contradicted, by something that is written
in the latter part of the Quran.

When one tries to construct the life and teaching of
Muhammad in a chronological order, he finds himself
jumping all over the Quran from one Sura to the other,
irrespective of the order in which the Suras are placed
in the Quran.

This, of course, causes tremendous confusion to
anyone who attempts to understand the Quran as a
piece of literature.

Dating The Suras

Since a religious leader tends to get long winded the
longer he ministers, most scholars believe that the
shortest Suras were no doubt the first ones Muhammad
preached and the longer Suras were the last. As time
went on, the Suras would get longer as he had more to
say.

But there is at times a mixture of Meccan and
Medinan revelations in the same Sura so that even size
is not an infallible guide in dating the Suras.

First Person

In terms of the way in which the Quran is written, the Muslims claim that the Quran is always in the first person speech in which Allah himself is speaking to man.

Such a claim, alas, does not fit the text of the Quran. There are many sections in which it is clear that Allah is not speaking, but someone else.

Endless Repetition

Another problem with the Quran is that since it was intended to be memorized by those who were illiterate and uneducated and thus could not read it, it engages in the principal of endless repetition of the same material over and over again.

Thus one will frequently encounter the same stories the same revelations in the Quran.

While this is no doubt helpful to the illiterate masses often found in the Muslim world, it does tend to irritate educated people.

The Right "Feel"

The last observation about the Quran as a whole is that is does not have the feeling that it is complete.

When you pick up the Bible, you find that it begins at the BEGINNING of all things, the creation of the heavens and the earth (Gen. 1:1).

As you proceed through the Bible, you learn in chronological order about the Fall of man into sin, the great Flood, the Tower of Babel, the calling of Abraham, the patriarchs, the calling of Moses, the Exodus, the building up of the nation, the ultimate captivity of the nation, the people going into exile, their return under Cyrus, the rebuilding of Israel, the prediction of the coming of the Messiah, the coming of the Messiah, His life, death, resurrection, and the beginning of the church age. Then when you come to the last book of the Bible, you read concerning the END of the universe.

Thus the Bible gives us a sense of wholeness or completeness for it begins at the BEGINNING and runs all the way through to the END of history.

No Beginning or End

But when you turn to the Quran, because of its jumbled and disordered condition, you are not left with that sense or feeling of completeness.

You are, as it were, left hanging after each Sura because there is no logical connection from one to the other.

For example, one Sura will deal with some pedantic matter such as Allah wants Muhammad's wife to stop arguing and bickering in his presence while the next Sura attacks of the idols of the Arabians.

Thus you are left with a feeling of incompleteness and dissatisfaction that you are not getting the whole story.

Conclusion

If one were to contrast the 66 books of the Bible written over a period of several thousand years by at least 40 different authors with the Quran which came through one man, Muhammad, during his lifetime, there would be no contest as to which was the superior literature.

The fact that the Quran claims that it is a continuation of the Old and New Testament is actually damaging to the Muslim cause because the Quran, in the final analysis, simply does not fit the literary style or structure that is found in the Old and New Testament.

To go from the Bible to the Quran is to go from the superior to the inferior, from the greater to the lesser, from the real to the counterfeit.

Footnotes

1. Quoted by Professor H. A. Gibb in Mohammedanism, An Historical Survey, ibid., p. 37.

2. Salmon, Reinach, Orpheus: A History Of Religion, (Livercraft, Inc., N.Y., 1932) p. 176.

3. Edward, Gibbon, The Decline and Fall of the Roman Empire, (Milman Co., London, n.d.) I:365.

4. McClintock and Strong, ibid., V:151

5. Dashti, bid., p.28.

6. Concise Encyclopedia of Islam, ibid., p.231.

7. ibid., p. 230. See also: Guillaume, Islam, p. 57, etc..

8. Abdul, Mandudi, The Meaning Of The Quran, Islamic Pub. ltd., Lahore, 1967), p.17.

9. Mandudi, ibid., p.17.

10. Dashti, ibid., p.28.

9

Muslim Claims For
The Quran

The claims that Muslims make for the origin, history, composition and preservation of the text of the Quran are so startling that they must be examined.

Perfect Arabic
First, Muslims claim that the text of the Quran is written in perfect Arabic in every respect because Allah wrote it in heaven.

The Shorter Encyclopedia of Islam states, "To Muslims the absolute perfection of the language of the Koran is an impregnable dogma."[1]

Since whatever Allah does must be perfect, the Quran must be in perfect Arabic. This claim is found in Sura 12:2, 13:37; 41:41, 44.

A Table In Heaven
Second, Allah wrote the Quran in heaven on a stone tablet the size of a table before it was handed down to Muhammad.

No Variant Readings

Third, it is further claimed that because the Quran is perfect, there are no variant readings, lost verses or conflicting manuscripts on the text of the Quran.

At this point, Muslim apologists have pointed out that while the Bible has many conflicting readings on various texts, the Quran is perfect and thus has no variant readings.

The Originals Found

Fourth, many Muslims have told us with absolute confidence that the "original manuscript" of the Quran which Muhammad himself gathered and constructed is still in existence and all Qurans come from this one single original manuscript.

Fifth, because the Quran is in the language of Allah, no mortal man can translate it into another language.

Sixth, no one can write any literature like that found in the Quran. (Sura 10:37-38)

Are These Things So?

Are these claims true? Are they in accord with the facts? We have to state, quite unequivocally, that these claims are false.

Not Perfect Arabic

First of all, the Quran is not in perfect Arabic. It contains many grammatical errors, such as in Sura 2: 177,192; 3:59; 4:162; 5:69; 7:160; 13:28; 20:66; 63:10, etc.

Ali Dashti comments,

The Qor'an contains sentences which are incomplete and not fully intelligible without the aid of commentaries;

foreign words, unfamiliar Arabic words, and words used with other than the normal meaning; adjectives and verbs inflected without observance of the concords of gender and number; illogically and ungrammatically applied pronouns which sometimes have no referent; and predicates which in rhymed passages are often remote from the subjects.[2] To sum up, more than one hundred Qor'anic aberrations from the normal rules and structure of Arabic have been noted.[3]

Foreign Words

Secondly, there are parts of the Quran that are not even in the Arabic language!

In his book, The Foreign Vocabulary of the Quran, Arthur Jeffery documents the fact that the Quran contains over one hundred foreign (i.e. non-Arabic) words.[4]

There are Egyptian, Hebrew, Greek, Syrian, Akkadian, Ethiopian, and Persian words and phrases in the Quran. It is thus not all Arabic.

The Middle East scholar, Canon Sell pointed out,

The number of foreign words is very great. They are borrowed from many languages. In the Mutawakkil by Jalalu's-Din as-Syuti one hundred and seven words are enumerated and commented on. This valuable book has been translated by W. Y. Bell, Yale University. The Arabic text is also given. It incidentally shows how many ideas have been borrowed.[5]

Many Variant Readings

Thirdly, the Muslims attack the Bible on the grounds that it sometimes has conflicting wording from different manuscripts.

Yet, this is exactly the case with the text of the Quran. There are many conflicting readings on the text of the Quran as Author Jeffery has demonstrated in his book, Material for the History of the Text of the Quran.[6]

At one point, Jeffery gives 90 pages of variant readings on the text. For example, in Sura 2, there are over 140 conflicting and variant readings on the text of the Quran.

All Western and Muslim scholars admit the presence of variant readings in the text of the Quran.[7]

Guillaume points out that the Quran at first, "had a large number of variants, not always trifling in significance."[8]

It is interesting to note that in scholarly Muslim journals, there is beginning to be a grudging acknowledgement of the fact that there are variant and conflicting readings on the text of the Quran.[9]

A Muslim Cover Up

The work of Western scholars such as Arthur Jeffery and others has been hampered by Muslim reluctance to let Western scholars see old manuscripts of the Quran which are based on pre-Uthman texts. Jeffery relates one incident.

An interesting modern example occurred during the last visit of the late Prof. Berstrasser to Cairo. He was engaged in taking photographs for the Archive and had photographed a number of the early Kufic Codices in the Egyptian Library when I drew his attention to one in the Azhar Library that possessed certain curious features.

He sought permission to photograph that also, but permission was refused and the Codex withdrawn from access, as it was not consistent with orthodoxy to allow a Western scholar to have knowledge of such a text.[10]

Jeffery comments, "With regard to such variants as did survive there were definite efforts at suppression in the interests of orthodoxy."[11]

Some Verses Missing

Fourth, some of the original verses of the Quran were lost. For example, the Sura Al-Saff had 200 verses in the days of Ayesha, but by the time Uthman standardized the text of the Quran, it had only 52 verses left. A total of 128 had been lost and they have never been recovered.

Other Suras were lost as the individuals who retained them in their living memory died in battle before they could be committed to writing.

The Shiite Muslims claim that Uthman left out 25% of the original verses in the Quran for political reasons.[12]

That there are verses which were left out of Uthman's version of the Quran is universally recognized.[13]

John Burton's book, The Collection Of the Quran, which was published by Cambridge University, documents how such verses were lost.[14]

Burton states concerning the Muslim claim that the Quran is perfect,

The Muslim account of the history of the Quran Texts are a mass of confusion, contradiction and inconsistencies.[15]

Changes In The Quran

One interesting way that some of the original verses

of the Quran were lost is that a follower of Muhammad named Abdollah Sarh would make suggestions to Muhammad about rephrasing, adding or subtracting to the Suras. Muhammad often did as Sarh suggested.

Dashti explains what happened.

> Abdollah renounced Islam on the ground that the revelations, if from God, could not be changed at the prompting of a scribe such as he. After his apostasy he went to Mecca and joined the Qorayshites.[16]

It is no wonder that when Muhammad conquered Mecca one of the first people he had killed was Abdollah for he knew too much and opened his mouth too often.

Some Verses "Abrogated"

In another process, called "abrogation," verses which are contradictory to Muslim faith and practice have been removed from the text. The "satanic verses" in which Muhammad approved of the worship of the three goddesses, the daughters of Allah were removed for this reason.

The Arabic scholar E. Wherry comments,

> There being some passages in the Quran which are contradictory, the Muhammadan doctors obviate any objection from thence by the doctrine of abrogation; for they say that GOD in the Quran commanded several things which were for good reasons afterwards revoked and abrogated.[17]

Prof. Wherry goes on to document numerous examples of verses taken out of the Quran.

Canon Sell in his work, Historical Development of the Quran, stated concerning the practice of abrogating verses out of the Quran ,

> It is to us astounding how so compromising a procedure can have been permitted to be introduced into the system by friends and foes.[18]

Some Verses Added

Not only have parts of the Quran been lost, but entire verses and chapters have been added to it.

For example, Ubai had several Suras in his manuscript of the Quran which Uthman omitted from his standardized text.

Thus there were Qurans in circulation before Uthman's text which had additional revelations from Muhammad that Uthman did not find or approve of and thus he failed to place them in his text.

No Originals

As to the claim that the original manuscript of the Quran is still in existence, we have already pointed out there was no single "manuscript" of the Quran.

As Arthur Jeffery stated,

> Nothing is more certain than that when the Prophet died there was no collected, arranged, collated body of revelation. The earliest strata of tradition available to us make it quite certain that there was no Quran left ready as a heritage for the community. The Prophet had proclaimed his messages orally, and, except in the later period of his ministry, whether they were recorded or not was often a matter of chance.[19]

What about the Muslim claim that Muhammad had compiled a complete manuscript of the Quran before he died?

Jeffery answers, "Very little is needed to reveal the fact that this account is largely fictitious."[20]

Caesar Farah in his book on Islam, states, "When Muhammed died there existed no singular codex of the sacred text."[21]

The Shorter Encyclopedia Of Islam comments,

One thing only is certain and is openly recognized by tra-dition, namely, that there was not in existence any collection of revelations in final form, because, as long as he was alive, new revelations were being added to the earlier ones.[22]

It is clear therefore, that the bones, stones, palm leaves, tree bark, etc. which contained some of the material which Muhammad spoke after his seizures or trances was gathered together AFTER his death.

It is also a fact that none of these things are in existence today. They have all long since been lost or rotted away.

The early versions of the Quran were in conflict with each other. Some had more or fewer Suras than others. The wording was often different.

On each occasion when we challenged a Muslim apologist to tell us the place where the "original" manuscript of the Quran was stored, he stated that he did not know where it was but that he was sure that it existed because it had to. Such an argument is worse than no argument at all!

Uthman's Text

As to the labor of the Caliph Uthman, the following historical facts must be noted:

(1.) Why did he have to standardize a common text if a standard text was already in existence?

(2.) Why did he try to destroy all the "other" manuscripts if there were no other conflicting manuscripts?

(3.) Why did he have to use the threat of death to force people to accept his text if everyone had the same text?

(4.) Why did many people reject his text in favor of their own texts?

These four facts reveal the utter state of confusion and contradiction that existed in the time of Uthman over the text of the Quran.

The fact that he ordered that all the older copies of the Quran should be destroyed reveals his fear that such copies would reveal that his own text was deficient by either adding to or subtracting from what Muhammad actually said.

Thankfully, some of these older materials have survived and have been recovered by such scholars as Arthur Jeffery.

Western scholars have shown beyond all reasonable doubt that Uthman's text did not contain all of the Quran and neither was it correct in all of its wording in what it did contain.

Plenty Of Translations

As to the Muslim claim that the Quran cannot be translated, it is amazing to us that the English Muslim

Mohammed Pickthal could state, "The Koran cannot be translated" (p.vii), in the very introduction to his excellent translation of it!

The claim that the Quran cannot be translated is clearly refuted by the existence of many such translations.

Suras Like It Written

The challenge to produce Suras like those found in the Quran has been answered several times. The Middle East scholar Canon Sell comments,

Men can produce its like in eloquence and arrangement. A man, named Nadir ibn Haritha, was bold enough to accept the challenge, and arranged some stories of the Persian kings in chapters and Suras and recited them.[23]

McClintock and Strong comment,

Hamzah ben-Ahed wrote a book against the Koran with at least equal elegance, and Maslema another, which surpassed it, and occasioned a defection of great number of Mussulmans.[24]

One last observation will be made in this chapter.

The Fingerprints Of Muhammad

Since Muslims claim that the Quran was "handed down" from Heaven, and that Muhammad cannot be viewed as its human author, it is interesting to point out that, according to the Concise Encyclopedia of Islam, the Arabic of the Quran is in the dialect and vocabulary of someone who was a member of the Quraysh tribe living in the city of Mecca. Thus Muhammad's fingerprints can be found all over the Quran.[25]

If the Quran was written in some kind of heavenly, perfect Arabic, why then does it clearly reveal that it was spoken by someone who was a member of the Quraysh tribe residing in Mecca?

We must submit that the argument of the Muslims that the Quran was written in heavenly Arabic falls to the ground. The Quran, in its dialect, vocabulary, and content, reflects the style of its author, Muhammad, not some heavenly Allah.

Conclusion

The true history of the collection and the creation of the text of the Quran reveals that the Muslim claims are indeed fictitious and not in accord with the facts. The fingerprints of Muhammad can be seen on every page as a witness to its human origin.

Footnotes

1. Shorter Encyclopedia of Islam, ibid., pgs. 276.

2. Dashti, ibid., pgs, 48.

3. ibid., p.50

4. Arthur Jeffery, The Foreign Vocabulary of The Quran, (Oriental Institute, Baroda, 1938, no. 79)

5. Edward, Sell, Studies In Islam, ibid., p. 226.

6. Arthur Jeffery, Materials For The History Of The Text Of The Quran, (Russell F. Moore, N.Y., 1952)

7. Dashti, p. 28; Mandudi, pgs. 17-18; McClintock and Strong, V:152;

8. Guillaume, Islam, ibid, p. 189.

9. One example would be Saleh al-Wahaihu, "A Study Of Seven Quranic Variants" (International Journal Of Islamic and Arabic Studies, vol. V, (1989), no.2, pgs. 1-57.

10. Jeffery, Materials, p. 10, n.2.

11. ibid., p. 9

12. McClintock and Strong, V:152.

13. Shorter Encyclopedia of Islam, pgs., 278-282; Guillaume, Islam, p. 191; Wherry, pgs. 110-111, etc.

14. John, Burton, The Collection of The Quran, (Cambridge University Press, London, 1977), pgs. 117f. See also: Arthur, Jeffery, Islam: Muhammad And His Religion, (The Liberal Arts Press, N.Y., 1958), pgs. 66-68.

15. Burton, p.231.

16. Dashti, pgs. 98

17. E. M. Wherry, A Comprehensive Commentary On The Quran, ibid., p. 110.

18. Cannon, Sell, Historical Development of The Quran, (Diocesan Press, Madras, 1923), pgs. 36-37.

19. Jeffery, Materials, pgs. 5-6. See also Caesar Farah, p. 28.

20. Jeffery, ibid.

21. Caesar, Farah, Islam: Beliefs and Observations, (Barrons, N.Y., 1987) p.28.

22. Shorter Encyclopedia Of Islam, ibid., p. 271.

23. Sell, Studies, ibid., p.208.

24. McClintock and Strong, ibid., V:152.

25. Concise Encyclopedia of Islam, p. 228.

10

A Scientific Examination Of The Quran

It never ceases to amaze us that many modern Muslims feel that they have the perfect right and freedom to criticize the Bible as being corrupt and contradictory but whenever anyone dares to criticize the Quran along the same lines, they label this as rude and offensive!

Bucaille's Book

One example of this is Bucaille's book, The Bible, The Quran and Science. While he launches a full scale attack on the inspiration and text of the Bible, when it comes to the Quran, he assures the reader that it has "undisputed authenticity!" Thus he does not deal with the many problems found in the Quran but spends his time attacking the Bible[1].

In reality, people have been "disputing" the Quran from the very beginning and are still disputing it today.

Several Problems

There are several problems with Bucaille's methodology.

First, both the Quran and the Hadith uphold the Bible as the inspired Word of God and frequently appeal to it as the authority for what Muhammad taught and did. Thus if the Bible is brought down, then the Quran and the Hadith will go down with it.[2]

Second, Bucaille violates one of the most basic laws of logic. Indeed, his book bristles with every logical error known to man. But, in particular, he assumes that if he can "refute" the Bible, then the Quran is established. But this is totally illogical. You cannot prove your own position by simply refuting some one else's position.

As a matter of logic, the Bible, the Quran and the Hadith could all be wrong! The Quran is not inspired just because some other scared book is refuted. Each book must stand or fall on its own merits.

Circular Reasoning

Some Muslims at this point use circular reasoning when it comes to the Quran. They assert as true what they have yet to prove.

Muslim: Muhammad was the prophet of God.
Non-Muslim: Why is this true?
Muslim: The Quran says so.
Non-Muslim: Why is the Quran true?
Muslim: Muhammad was the prophet of God.

Muslim: The Quran is without error.

Non-Muslim: Why is this true?
Muslim: Because the Quran says so.
Non-Muslim: But why is the Quran true?
Muslim: The Quran is without error.

Instead of endlessly rowing in a circle with only one oar, we must submit the Quran to a critical scientific examination. If it is true, it will stand up to any examination. But if it is false, it is better to know it now than to take a blind leap of faith.

The Gospel Of Barnabas

The recent attempt of some Muslims to use the gnostic work entitled, The Gospel Of Barnabas as if it were a long "lost" gospel by the disciple that bears its name and more authoritative than the New Testament, deserves a few comments.

Western scholars have repeatedly demonstrated that the so-called Gospel of Barnabas is a fraud in every respect.[3] For example, Barnabas did not write it because it's vocabulary reveals that it was not written in the first century.

Most importantly, it contains statements that clearly contradict the teachings found in the Quran, the Hadith and the Bible! It is a sword that cuts three ways!

Thus, just as the Muslim can use this so-called "lost" gospel to contradict the Bible, non-muslims can also use it to contradict the Quran and the Hadith.[4]

For example, The Gospel of Barnabas condemns having more than one wife while the Quran allows up to four wives. It also allows the eating of pork while the Quran condemns it.

For a Muslim to proclaim the inspiration of the Gospel of Barnabas is to put a knife to his own throat!

Freedom To Criticize

What Muslims must understand is that if they have the freedom to criticize the Bible, than other people have the same freedom to criticize the Quran. After all, "What is sauce for the gander is also sauce for the goose!"

We must introduce the material in this chapter in this way because of countless encounters with irate Muslims who felt that any criticism of the Quran is blasphemous and should not be allowed.

This insight explains why some Muslim apologists will never agree to debate the errors and the contradictions in the Quran. They will only want to debate Christianity, the Bible, etc. but never to defend the Quran itself.

Agreement Ahead Of Time

After years of dealing with Muslims, we have found it essential at the outset to get their agreement to the fact that in the West we have religious freedom which means that we have the right to criticize the Bible, the Quran, the Hadith, the Vedas, the Book of Mormon and any other "holy" book.

Not A Personal Slur

Such discussions should not be viewed as a personal attack or slur. They should be carried out in an objective and scholarly manner in order that the truth may be discovered.

Any religion which refuses to allow people to examine its sacred book using the normal rules of research and logic evidently has something to hide.

The Plain Truth

The plain truth is that the Quran contains many problems some of which we will now point out.

Since the Quran claims to be free from all error as proof of its inspiration in Sura 85:21-22, the presence of just one error in the Quran is enough to cast serious doubt on that claim.

The Bible vs The Quran

Throughout his early ministry, Muhammad constantly appealed to the Old and New Testament Scriptures as the basis and standard by which his teachings should be judged.

Thus he would say that if you wanted to know whether he was speaking the truth, go ask the people of the Book and ask them to look in their Scriptures to see whether or not what he was saying was true: Suras 2-13, 16-17, 20-21,23, 25-26, 28-29, 32, 34-35,39-48, 53-54, 61-62, 66, 74, 80, 87, 98, etc.

The Principle Was Sound

The principle that Muhammad used in the beginning was a valid one. The older revelation must be the judge of all so-called new revelations. Thus the Bible must be the standard which judges all new revelations including the Quran itself.

This is simply a point of chronology. Muhammad came 600 years after Jesus Christ. The Quran thus came AFTER the completion of the New Testament.

The Old Verified The New

The validity of the New Testament is based upon the

fact of its fulfillment of the predictions, symbolism, and typology of the Old Testament.

In the same way, if the Quran is to be received as the word of God, it must meet the test of being in complete compliance and accord with the Holy Scriptures as found in the Bible.

The Quran itself claims that it is a continuation of the Bible and it will not contradict it. (Sura 2:136)

A Point Of Logic

What this means in logic is that whenever the Bible and the Quran have a conflict or contradiction, the Quran is to give way, not the Bible.

This is particularly true when the text of the Quran contradicts the text of the Bible. The Muslim position is that the SAME God (Allah) revealed the Bible and the Quran. Thus the Quran will never contradict the Bible. Otherwise Allah would be contradicting himself.

It is only obvious that if Allah contradicted himself, he is not perfect. And, if he is not perfect, then he cannot be God.

A Literary Comparison

This calls for a literary comparison of the text of the Bible and the text of the Quran.

It is not even necessary for someone to believe in the inspiration of the Bible to make a comparison between it and the Quran.

Logically speaking, an atheist, skeptic, Hindu or Jew could make such a literary comparison just as well as a committed Christian.

Which Book Has Priority?

If the Quran does not correspond to the text and

teachings of the Bible, then the Quran contradicts the Bible. If it contradicts the Bible, then the Quran comes out the loser. Why?

Since the Bible was BEFORE the Quran and it appeals to the Bible for verification, then, whenever there is a conflict between the two, the newer and the lesser (i.e. the Quran) must give way to the older and the greater (i.e. the Bible).

Is The Bible Corrupt?

The Muslim answer to this approach is to say that the Quran is always right even when it disagrees with the Bible. Why? Because the Bible has been corrupted and cannot be trusted.

Now, while it is easy to say that the text of the Bible is corrupt, it is another thing to prove it.

In countless encounters with Muslims, whenever the Quran contradicts some particular verse in the Bible, they have always said, "The Bible is corrupted at this point."

Now, when I ask for some kind of proof that this Hebrew or Greek text is "corrupt," they respond by saying, "I do not have to prove it is corrupt. It has to be corrupt otherwise it would agree with the holy Quran."

This is circular reasoning once again. For example, the Quran contradicts the Bible in that it denies that Jesus was crucified.

Now, is there any manuscript evidence that the verses in the Bible which speak of Christ's crucifixion were not originally in the Bible? Is there any textual evidence of any kind whatsoever that the Bible did not originally teach the crucifixion?

There is no evidence whatsoever that the biblical text was corrupted on the crucifixion. The Bible from the beginning clearly taught that Jesus died on the cross.[5]

A Logical Dilemma

The Muslim is trapped at this point. If he admits that the Bible originally said that Jesus died on the cross, then the Quran is in direct conflict with the older revelations.

But Muhammad promised that this would not happen. Why? The Quran must agree with the older revelations because they all supposedly came from the same God.

On the one hand, if he rejects the Bible, he has to also reject the Quran because it appeals to the Bible as God's Word.

On the other hand, if he accepts the Bible, he still must reject the Quran because it contradicts the Bible. Either way, the Quran loses.

A Blind Leap Of Faith

So what does he do? He takes a blind leap of faith and says, "The text of the Bible at this place must be corrupted. It did not originally teach that Jesus was crucified. I do not have to prove it so. I know it is so because otherwise I am trapped and I will have to give up the Quran because it appeals to the Bible as the basis of its own authority."

The illogic and unreasonableness of the Muslim's argument grates against the scientific mind.

If there is not a shred of evidence that a particular text in the Bible has suffered any manuscript corruption, then it is irrational to say that it is corrupt just because it disagrees with the Quran.

Muslims answer this problem by saying that the Bible was corrupted AFTER the Quran was written.

But since we have manuscripts of the O.T. from as early as 200 B.C. and portions of the N.T. from the 1st century, we KNOW what the Bible was like during the life of Jesus and the apostles.

When we compare this uncorrupted Bible with the mixed up accounts, names and speeches found in the Quran, the Quran is shown to be false.

It must also be pointed out that the Muslims argue that the Quran must be perfect because God would preserve His word infallibly. Yet, if God failed to do this for the Bible — as they claim — why should He do this for the Quran?

A Scientific Examination

With these few introductory words, we will now proceed to a scientific examination of the Quran.

Since the Quran has so many problems, we will limit ourselves to around one hundred of the most obvious ones.

How Many Days Of Creation?

The very first problem in the Quran concerns the number of days it took God to create the world.

The Quran says that it took God EIGHT days to create the world when you add up all the days mentioned in Sura 41:9,10,12. (4 days + 2 days + 2 days = 8 days)

But it only took SIX days according to the Bible (Gen. 1:31). Thus the Quran begins its contradiction of the Bible in the very first chapter of the Bible.

When a Muslim friend objected to this, he stated that the Hebrew text of the Bible was no doubt corrupted at this point and that it originally said that the creation took eight days.

I pointed out that there was no evidence in the Hebrew manuscripts of any corruption. Also, the Bible elsewhere says that the world was created in six days! (Exo. 20:8)

Then I pointed out that the Quran in Sura 7:51 and 10:3 agreed with the biblical account that the creation of the world only took six days. Thus the Quran is in deep trouble either way.

If six days is wrong, then the Quran in Sura 7 and 10 is wrong. But if eight days is wrong, then Sura 41 is wrong. Either way the Quran loses. Using classic Muslim circular reasoning, he responded that then the Quran did not say eight days.

I added up the days mentioned in Sura 41 as 4+2+2=8.

He then added it up and came up with 4+2+2=6 "because 4 is divisible by 2 and hence 4 is actually a 2!"

When I pointed out that the Arabic said 4 and not 2, it did not phase him. He argued that 4=2 otherwise he would be trapped into having to admit that the Quran was in error.

Thus he made the utterly ridiculous statement that 4=2 rather than simply accepting the fact that Muhammad made an error at this point.

Noah, the Flood and His Sons

According to the Bible, all three sons of Noah went into the ark with him and were saved from the Flood

(Gen. 7:1,7,13).

Yet, the Quran in Sura 11:32-48 says that one of the sons refused to go into the ark and was drowned in the flood!

Sura 11:44 also claims that the Ark came to rest on top of Mt. Judi while the Bible says Mt. Ararat. These contradictions cannot be clearer.

Mistakes About Abraham

The Quran makes many errors concerning Abraham:

a. The Quran says that his father's name was Azar but the Bible says his name was Terah (Sura 6:74).

b. He did not live and worship in the valley of Mecca (Sura 14:37) but in Hebron according to the Bible.

c. It was his son Isaac that he went to sacrifice and not Ishmael as the Quran says. (Sura 37:100-112)

d. He had eight sons and not just two as the Quran claims.

e. He had three wives and not two as the Quran says.

f. He did not build the Kabah even though the Quran says so in Sura 2:125-127.

g. He was not thrown into a fire by Nimrod as the Quran claims in Sura 21:68-69 and 9:69.

This last error is most serious because it reveals a very frequent problem in the Quran.

Nimrod lived many centuries before Abraham. Thus they did not live at the same time. How then did Nimrod manage to throw Abraham into a fire when Nimrod had been dead for centuries?

Linear Time

The 7th century Arab and Muhammad in particular,

did not think in terms of linear time, i.e. historical chronology.

In the West, people think of history in terms of a straight line with a beginning, a middle, and an end.

In the East people think of time in terms of never ending cycles and not a straight line.

Evidently, in the Middle East at the time of Muhammad, Arabs did not have any settled conception of time.

Arab stories and legends would put together places, people and events in one present vision as if they were all living at the same time!

This is why throughout the Quran, Nimrod and Abraham, Haman and Moses, Mary and Aaron, etc. were all pictured as living and working together.

This is why the Quran can put together the Flood and Moses, the Tower of Babel and Pharoah, etc., as if all those things happened at the same time.

This is a very serious challenge to the integrity of the Quran because its violates the historical chronology of the Bible and secular history at the same time.

Mistakes About Joseph

The Quran makes the mistake of saying that the man who bought Joseph was named Aziz (Sura 12:21f) when his name was really Potiphar (Gen. 37:36).

Biblical Characters

The Quran makes the same kind of error when it refers to Goliath as Jalut, Korah as Karun, Saul as Talut, Enoch as Idris, Ezekiel as Dhu'l-Khifl, John the

Baptist as Yahya, Jonah as Yunus, etc.

Muhammad did not have access to the Bible because an Arabic translation of the Bible was not in existence at that time. Thus he frequently got the names, events and chronology all wrong.

As pagan, Jewish and Christian traders sat around the fire telling each other their favorite stories, they would get the names, times and events all jumbled up and confused.

The Encyclopedia Britannica states,

> The deviations from the biblical narratives are very marked, and can in most cases be traced back to the legendary anecdotes of the Jewish Haggada and the Apocryphal Gospels. Much has been written concerning the sources from which Mohammed derived this information; there is no evidence that he was able to read, and his dependence on oral communication may explain some of his misconceptions; e.g., the confusion of Haman, the minister of Ahasuerus, with the minister of Pharoah (xl,38), and the identification of Miriam, the sister of Moses, with Mary (Miriyam), the mother of Jesus.[6]

Muhammad's gross misunderstandings of biblical stories and doctrines reflect only a hearsay knowledge. As the great Arabic scholar Cannon Edward Sell pointed out concerning these erroneous names, "He certainly did not get them from the Old Testament. The confusion of names is quite remarkable."[7]

Mistakes About Moses

The Quran contains many errors concerning Moses.

a. It was not Pharoah's wife who adopted Moses as

the Quran claims in Sura 28:8-9. It was actually
Pharoah's daughter (Exo. 2:5).

b. Noah's flood did not take place in Moses' day
(Sura 7:136 cf. 7:59f). This goof cannot be easily
swept aside!

c. The Quran says that Haman lived in Egypt during
the time of Moses and worked for Pharoah building the
Tower of Babel! (Surah 27:4-6; 28:38; 29:39; 40:23-
24,36-37) But Haman actually lived in Persia and was
in the service of King Ahauerus. See the Book of
Esther for details.[8] This is a very serious error as it not
only contradicts the Bible but secular history as well.

d. Crucifixion was not used in the time of Pharoah
although the Quran says so in Sura 7:124.

Mistakes About Mary

The Quran contains many errors concerning Mary,
the mother of Jesus:

a. Her father's name was not Imram (Sura 66:12).

b. She did not give birth to Jesus under a Palm tree
but in a stable. (Sura 19:22 vs Luke 2:1-20).

c. Muhammad confused the mother of Jesus with
the Miriam who was the sister of Moses and Aaron
(Sura 19:28).[9] This is a very serious error as it reveals
that Muhammad had no understanding of the
different time periods for biblical figures.

d. He clearly made up fraudulent speeches and
miracles for her in Sura 19:23-26.

e. Zacharias could not speak the entire time until his
son was born, not just for three days as the Quran
claims. (Sura 19:10 vs. Luke 1:20)

Fictional Speeches

Muhammad made up fictional speeches of people in the Bible using such words as "Muslim" and "Islam" which were not in the languages of the people supposedly quoted at that time.

This would be as ridiculous as claiming that Muhammad said, "I like Kentucky Fried Chicken best."

Obviously, such terminology did not exist in Muhammad's time! And neither did the terminology Muhammad put into the mouth of biblical figures.

In the same way, all the speeches attributed to Abraham, Isaac, Jacob, Noah, Moses, Mary, Jesus, etc. contain words and phrases which clearly reveal that they are all frauds: Sura 2:60, 126-128, 132-133, 260; 3:49-52, 67; 6:74-82; 7:59-63, 120-126; 10:71-72; 18:60-70; 19:16-33, etc..

The Water Test

The test of how the soldiers drank water from a stream did not take place in the days of Saul when David defeated Goliath but many years earlier with Gideon. Compare Sura 2:249-250 with Judges 7:1-8.

Secular History Mistakes

The Quran contains clear historical mistakes.

a. One example would be in Sura 105 where Muhammad claimed that the elephant army of Abrah was defeated by birds dropping stones of baked clay upon them.

According to the historical record, Abrah's army withdrew their attack on Mecca after small-pox broke out among the troops.[10]

b. The Kabah was not built by Adam and then rebuilt

by Abraham. It was built by pagans to worship a black rock which fell out of the sky. Abraham never lived at Mecca.

c. In Sura 20:87,95 we are told the Jews made the golden calf in the wilderness at the suggestion of "the Samaritan."

This is a clear historical error as a people by that name did not exist during the time frame of the passage.

The Samaritans did not come into existence until AFTER the Captivity of Israel first by the Assyrians and then by the Babylonians.

Yusuf Ali tries to get away from this error by obscuring the translation of the name but the Arabic is clear.

d. One of the greatest errors in the Quran is concerning Alexander the Great who is mistakenly called Zul-qarnain.

The Quran claims that he was a Muslim who worshipped Allah and that he lived to an old age (Sura 18:89-98).

The indisputable fact of history is that Alexander was not a Muslim and he did not live to an old age.

This error is iron-clad as the historical evidence concerning Alexander is as clear.

The Encyclopedia Britannica states,

> His account of Alexander, introduced as "the two horned one" (xviii,82), is derived from the Romance of Alexander, which was current among the Nestorian Christians of the 7th Century in a Syriac version.[11]

In the light of this obvious historical error, some modern Muslims have argued that the Quran is not speaking of Alexander.

But even Yusuf Ali has to admit that based on the historic orthodox Muslim interpretation of this passage,

> I have not the least doubt that Zul-qarnain is meant to be Alexander the Great, the historic Alexander, and not some legendary Alexander.[12]

The Concise Dictionary of Islam also upholds the view that Alexander the Great is the subject in this passage.[13]

Scientific Problems

The Quran contains scientific errors. For example, it claims that a man wanted to find out where the sun went when it went down. So he followed the setting of the sun and found that it went down into the waters of a muddy spring!

The next day, the sun arose out of the waters. (Sura 18:85-86) This is absurd.

Self-Contradictions

The Quran contradicts itself in many ways. Since the Quran claims in Sura 39:23,28 to be free from all contradictions, just one contradiction is sufficient to show that it is not God's Word.

a. The Quran gives us four conflicting accounts of Muhammad's reception of the Quran:

1. We are first told that Allah came to Muhammad in the form of a man and that Muhammad saw him (Sura 53:2-18; 81:19-24).

2. Then we are told that it was "the holy Spirit" who

came to Muhammad (Sura 16:102; 26:192-194).

3. Later on, the Quran says that the angels were the ones who came down to Muhammad (Sura 15:8).

4. The last and most popular version is that it was the angel Gabriel who delivered the Quran to Muhammad (Sura 2:97). Which version is true?

b. The same quotation is given with conflicting wording. This is one of many such examples of this problem. (Sura 2:58 vs 7:161)

The presence of conflicting wording is serious because the Muslims claim that the Quran is absolutely perfect even in its quotations.

Christians do not make such claims for the Bible but view the speeches found in the Bible as summaries of what was said. Thus different Gospel writers summarized the sermons of Jesus in different words which is perfectly normal.

c. At first Muhammad told his followers to face Jerusalem in prayer. Then he told them since God was everywhere they could face any way they wanted. Then he changed his mind yet again and directed them to pray toward Mecca. (Sura 2:115 vs 2:144)

Many scholars believe that the change in direction took place depending on whether he was trying to please the Jews or the pagans.[14]

d. Muhammad first started out saying that his followers could defend themselves if attacked (Sura 22:39). Then he commanded them to go to war on his behalf (Sura 2:216-218). This was to gain wealth by robbing caravans. But as his army grew, so did his thirst for loot (Sura 5:33). So he ordered wars to persecute other religions as well as to gain more wealth (Sura 9:5, 29). Allah's will seem to change according to Muhammad's success in killing and looting.[15]

e. Who was the first to believe? Abraham or Moses? (Sura 6:14 vs 7:143) You can't have two "firsts."

f. The fact that Judaism and Christianity broke up into different sects was used in the Quran to prove that they were not of God. (Sura 30:30-32; 42:13-14)

Yet, Islam has itself broken up into many warring sects. Thus it too cannot be true if the Quran is right.

Convenient Revelations

The Quran contains convenient revelations for the personal gain or pleasure of Muhammad:

a. When Muhammad wanted his son-in-law's wife, he suddenly got a revelation from Allah declaring it right to take another man's wife (Sura 33:36-38).

b. When he wanted to stop his wives from quarreling or to accept more wives, he got a quick revelation for it (Sura 33:28-34).

c. When people bothered him at his house, he got a quick revelation setting up rules when to visit him and when not to bother him (Sura 33:53-58; 29:62-63; 49:1-5).

Legendary Materials

Muhammad used much legendary and fanciful material as sources for the Quran.[16]

As Prof. Jomier, one of France's greatest Middle East scholars, pointed out,

Moslems receive these narratives as the word of God, without inquiring about their historical background. In fact we have there a popular, poetic form of legends, variants of religious themes known from other sources.[17]

Arabian Sources

First, the Quran repeats fanciful Arabian fables as if they were true.

1. Arabic legends about the fabulous genies or jinns fill its pages.[18]

2. The story of the she-camel who leapt out of a rock and became a prophet was known long before Muhammad. (Sura 7:73-77,85; 91:14; 54:29)

3. The story of an entire village of people who were turned into apes because they broke the sabbath by fishing was a popular legend in Muhammad's day. (Sura 2:65; 7:163-166)

4. The gushing twelve springs story found in Sura 2:60 comes from pre-Islamic legends.

5. One of our favorite fables is what is called the "Rip Van Winkle story" of seven men and their animals who slept for 309 years in a cave and then woke up perfectly fine! (Sura 18:9-26) This legend is also found in Greek and Christian fables as well.

6. The fable of pieces of four dead, cut up birds getting up and flying was well known in Muhammad's time. (Sura 2:260)

Second, it is clear that Muhammad used the Saba Moallaqat of Imra'ul Cays in his composition of Suras 21:96; 29:31,46; 37:59; 54:1 and 93:1.

Jewish Sources

Many of the stories in the Quran come from the Jewish Talmud, the Midrash, and many apocryphal works.

This was pointed out by Abraham Geiger in 1833 in his pioneer article, "Was hat Mohammed us dem Judenthume aufgenommen?"

The evidence was brought up to date and further documented by another Jewish scholar, Dr. Abraham Katsh, of New York University, in 1954.[19]

1. The source of Sura 3:35-37 is the fanciful book called The Protevangelion's James The Lesser.

2. The source of Sura 87:19 is The Testament of Abraham.

3. The source of Sura 27:17-44 is the II Targum of Esther.

4. The fantastic tale that God made a man "die for a hundred years" with no ill effects on his food, drink or donkey was a Jewish fable (Sura 2:259f).

5. The idea that Moses was resurrected and other material came from the Jewish Talmud (Sura 2:55-56, 67).

6. The story in Sura 5:30-31 can also be found in pre-Islamic works from Pirke Rabbi Eleazer, the Targum of Jonathan ben Uzziah and the Targum of Jerusalem.

7. The tale of Abraham being delivered from Nimrod's fire came from the Midrash Rabbah. (see: Sura 21:51-71; 29:16-17; 37:97-98) It must be also pointed out that Nimrod and Abraham did not live at the same time. Muhammad was always mixing people together in the Quran who did not live at the same time.

8. The non-biblical details of the visit of the Queen Of Sheba (Saba) in Sura 27:20-44 came from the II Targum of the Book Of Esther.

9. The source of Sura 2:102 is no doubt the Midrash Yalkut (ch. 44).

10. The story found in Sura 7:171 of God lifting up Mt. Sinai and holding it over the heads of the Jews as a threat to squash them if they rejected the law came from the Jewish book Abodah Sarah.

11. The story of the making of the golden calf in the

wilderness in which the image jumped out of the fire fully formed and actually mooed (Sura 7:148; 20:88) came from Pirke Rabbi Eleazer.

12. The seven heavens and hells described in the Quran came from the Zohar and the Hagigah.

13. Muhammad utilized the Testament of Abraham to teach that a scale or balance will be used on the day of judgement to weigh good and bad deeds in order to determine whether one went to heaven or hell (Sura 42:17;101:6-9).

Heretical Christian Sources

One of the most documented and damaging facts about the Quran is that Muhammad used heretical "Christian" Gnostic gospels and their fables for material in the Quran.

The Encyclopedia Britannica comments, ''The gospel was known to him chiefly through apocryphal and heretical sources.''[20]

This has been demonstrated many times by various scholars[21]. For example, in Sura 3:49 and 100:110, the baby Jesus speaks from the cradle! Later on, the Quran has Jesus making clay birds come alive!

The Bible tells us that the FIRST miracle Jesus did was at the wedding at Cana (John 2:11). The contradiction cannot be ignored.

Sabean Sources

Muhammad incorporated parts of the religion of the Sabeans into Islam[22].

He adopted such pagan rituals as:

1. Worshipping at the Kabah;

2. Praying five times a day toward Mecca; (Muhammad chose five of the same times the Sabeans prayed.)

3. Fasting for part of a day for an entire month; etc.

Eastern Religious Sources

Muhammad derived some of his ideas from Eastern religions such as Zoroastrianism and Hinduism. All of these things were in existence long before Muhammad was born.

The Quran records the following things which are ascribe to Muhammad but in reality are previously known stories now attributed to him for the first time.[23]

1. The story of a flying trip through seven heavens;
2. The Houries of paradise;
3. Azazil and other spirits coming up from Hades;
4. The "light" of Muhammad;
5. The bridge of Sirat;
6. Paradise with its wine, women and song comes from the Persians;
7. The king of death;
8. The peacock story.

Mistakes About Jesus

It contradicts the Bible's teaching on the person and work of Jesus Christ by saying in Sura 4:157; 5:19, 75; 9:30:

a. Jesus was not the Son of God.
b. He did not die for our sins.
c. He was not crucified.
d. He was not God as well as human.
e. He is not the Savior.[24]

The utter contradiction between the biblical and quranic view of Jesus cannot be dismissed so easily. This is clearly not an issue of corruption but of contradiction. It is one of the fundamental issues which will forever divide Christians from Muslims.

Mistakes About The Trinity

The Quran contains many errors about what Christians believe and practice. One of the most significant is that the Quran misrepresents the Christian doctrine of the Trinity.

Muhammad mistakenly thought that Christians worshipped three gods: the Father, the Mother (Mary) and the Son (Jesus) (Sura 5:73-75, 116).[25]

As Richard Bell pointed out, Muhammad never understood the doctrine of the Trinity.[26]

The Encyclopedia Britannica states that there are, "mistaken concepts of the Trinity in the Quran."[27]

Yusuf Ali's translation of the Quran tries to avoid this error by deliberately mistranslating Sura 5:73.

The Arabic text condemns those who say that "Allah is one of three" i.e. Allah is only one of three gods! Both Arberry and Pickthall translate this correctly.

Ali mistranslates Sura 5:73 to read, "They do blaspheme who say: God is one of three in a Trinity. "

The words "in a Trinity" are not in the Arabic text. Ali puts it in his translation in an attempt to avoid the rather obvious error that Christians believe in three gods.

In reality, Christians believe only in one God who is in three persons: the Father, the Son, and the Holy Spirit. They do not believe that Mary is a part of the Trinity.

Even The Concise Dictionary of Islam admits that,

In some cases the "material" which forms the substance of Quranic narrative, details of the creeds of Christianity and Judaism for example, does not correspond to those religion's own understanding of their beliefs. This could be said, for example, of the notion of the Trinity found in the Quran, the story of Satan's refusal to bow down to Adam, the Docetist view of the crucifixion, all of which can be traced to the dogmas of Gnostic sects, which are heretical in relationship to orthodox Christianity and Judaism. The Trinity "seen" in the Quran is not the Trinity of the Apostles Creed, or of the Nicene Creed.[28]

The Quran is so clearly erroneous at this point that Muslims such as Yusuf Ali must mistranslate the Quran to get away from it!

Mistakes About the "Son" of God
The Quran also makes the mistake of saying that Christians believe that Jesus is the "Son" of God in the sense that God the "Father" has a male body and had sexual intercourse with Mary.

In Muhammad's mind, to say that God has a son was to blaspheme because it would mean that God had sex with a woman (Sura 2:116; 6:100-101; 10:68; 16:57; 19:35; 23:91; 37:149, 157; 43:16-19).

Christians believe that Mary was a virgin when Jesus was conceived in her by the Holy Spirit (Luke 1:35).

Thus Jesus is the "Son" of God in a figurative sense-not a literal, sexual sense. God the "Father" is not a man and hence does not have a male body and has not had sex with anyone. The Quran is 100% wrong on this issue.

Praying Toward Jerusalem
The Quran makes the mistake of teaching that Christians bow in prayer toward Jerusalem (Sura 2:144-

145). Christians do not bow toward any place on earth when in prayer.

Is Allah the Name Of Christ?

Christians do not claim that Allah is the name of the Messiah or the Christ as Sura 5:72 claims. They believe in one God in three persons and that Jesus Christ was human as well as divine.

Mistakes About Jewish Beliefs

The Quran makes the mistake of claiming that the Jews believed that Ezra was the Son of God, i.e. the Messiah, just as Christians claim that Jesus was (Sura 9:30). This is absurd.

As The Concise Dictionary Of Islam points out, "There are many details regarding Judaism which are in variance with Jewish belief."[29]

Arab Racism

According to the literal Arabic of Sura 3:106-107, on the Judgment Day, only people with white faces will be saved. People with black faces will be damned. This is racism in its worst form!

As the Khalils pointed out in their article on Islam,

American blacks have been widely wooed by Islam, but through misinformation. They hear, "Christianity is the white man's religion; Islam is the religion of all mankind." They are told that Allah and Mohammed are black. In reality, Muslims in the Middle East still regard blacks as slaves. It would be worse than blasphemy for them to believe that either Allah or Mohammed were black.[30]

It must be also pointed out that Arab Muslims were enslaving black Africans long before Westerners to their shame got involved.

A Carnal Heaven

The Quran promises a heaven full of wine and free sex (Sura 2:25; 4:57;11:23; 47:15).

If the drinking of wine and gross immorality is sinful on earth, how is it right in Paradise?

Is this not yet more proof that Islam reflects the ideas and customs of 7th century Arab culture?

The Quran's picture of paradise is exactly what a 7th century pagan Arab would have thought wonderful.

The concept of a harem of beautiful women and all the wine you can drink is in direct conflict with the spirituality and holiness of the biblical concept of heaven (Rev. 22:12-17). The contradiction cannot be clearer.

The Problem Of Usury

In 7th century Arabia, the practice of charging interest on the money that you loaned to people was condemned as usury. Thus, it is no surprise to learn that Muhammad likewise condemned usury in the Quran (Sura 2:275ff; 3:130; 4:161; 30:39).

The reason that we point this out is that modern Muslims openly disobey the Quran at this point. Thus Muslims will charge interest on the money they loan and they will pay interest on the money that they borrow.

If the Muslims were to apply the Quran's condemnation of usury to their modern day financial practices, there would be no Muslim banks and not even Muslim governments could charge interest or receive interest on any loans.

This is why some Muslim apologists try desperately to stay clear of the issue of usury or they try to define it as taking unjust interest.

But it is clear, not only from the Quran, but also from the historical context, that Muhammad was denying the charging of any interest at all on money when it is loaned particularly to those who are fellow Muslims.

An Interesting Discussion

In one conversation with a Muslim, when I brought up the Quran's condemnation of charging interest on the money lent out to others, he dismissed this because he claimed that the Quran at that point was only reflecting 7th century Arabian culture and thus could be disregarded!

Then I pointed out that if this same principle was applied to all the other cultural elements within Islam, such as the five pillars, civil laws, dietary laws, dress codes, etc., Islam itself would collapse like a house of cards. He then stated that the Quran's condemnation of usury was not a "cultural" law but the eternal law of Allah.

Of course, I could not help but point out that he "cannot have his cake and eat it too." The Quran's condemnation of usury was either cultural and hence could be disobeyed or it was the eternal word of Allah and he would have to give up any interest bearing accounts he had.

To this he gave no response.

It is clear that every time a Muslim accepts interest payments on his bank accounts, loans, mortgages, etc., he is demonstrating to one and all that Islam and the Quran are really the products of 7th century Arabian culture and not the eternal word of God.

Conclusion

While the devout Muslim believes with all of his heart that the rituals and doctrines of Islam are entirely heavenly in origin and thus cannot have any earthly sources, Middle East scholars have demonstrated beyond all doubt that every ritual and belief in Islam can be traced back to pre-Islamic Arabian culture.

In other words, Muhammad did not preach anything new. They had all been believed and practiced in Arabia long before he was ever born. Even the idea of "only one God" was borrowed from the Jews and the Christians.

This irrefutable fact casts to the ground the Muslim claim that Islam was revealed from heaven. Since its rituals, beliefs and even the Quran itself can be fully explained in terms of pre-Islamic sources in Arabian culture, this means that the religion of Islam is false.

It is no surprise therefore that Western scholars have concluded that Allah is not God, Muhammad was not his prophet and the Quran is not the Word of God.

Footnotes

1. Bucaille, Maurice, The Bible, The Quran and Science, (American Trust Pub., Ind., 1979), p.126. He has been answered in a definitive way by Dr. William Campbell in a book soon to be published by Arab World Ministries in Upper Darby, Pa.. He was kind enough to allow us to read his unpublished manuscript.

2. For a short discussion of this point see: Ghiyathuddin, Adelphi and Ernest, Hahn, The Integrity of the Bible according to the Quran and the Hadith, (Henry Martyn Institute Of Islamic Studies, Hyderbad, India, 1977). John, Gilchrist, The Textual History of the Quran and the Bible, (Jesus To The Muslims, Benoni, South Africa, 1987). For a lengthy discussion see: C. G., Pfander, The Balance Of Truth, (Religious Tract Society, London, 1910).

3. Selim, Abdul-Ahad and Ernest, Hahn, The Gospel Of Barnabas, (Henry Martyn Institute of Islamic Studies, Hyderbad, India, 1985).

William, Campbell, The Gospel of Barnabas: Its True Value, Christian Study Center, Rawalpinidi, Pakistan, 1989). John, Gilchrist, Origins And Sources Of The Gospel Of Barnabas, (Jesus To The Muslims, Benoni, South Africa, 1987).

4. For a complete list of contradictions between the Quran and the Gospel Of Barnabas see Campbell, Abdul-Ahad and Hahn listed above.

5. For a short treatment on the subject see: John Gilchrist, The Crucifixion: A Fact, Not a Fiction, (Jesus To The Muslims, Benoni, South Africa, 1987). For a lengthy treatment see: Josh, McDowell and John, Gilchrist, The Islam Debate, (Here's Life Pub., San Berdino, Ca., 1983). Anis, Shorrosh, Islam Revealed, (Thomas Nelson, Nashville, 1988).

6. Encyclopedia Britannica, 15:479.

7. Sell, Edward, Studies In Islam, (Diocesan Press, Madras, 1928), p. 225.

8. C. G., Pfander, Balance Of Truth, ibid., pp.283f.

9. Caesar, Farah, Islam: Beliefs and Observations, (Barrons, N.Y., 1987), pp. 86f.

10. Guillaume, Islam, ibid., pp.21f.

11. Encyclopedia Britannica, 15:479.

12. Yusuf Ali, ibid, p. 763.

13. The Concise Dictionary of Islam, p. 229.

14. McClintock and Strong, ibid., VI:407. See also Dashti, ibid., p. 92.

15. Dashti, ibid., pp. 82f.

16. For the documentation on the sources of the Quran see the books listed in the bibliography under such names as Jeffery, Katsh, Tisdall, Gibb, Bell, Sell, Muir, Guillaume, Preserved Smith, Pfander, Shorrosh, Sweetman, Seale, Zwemer, as well as the standard reference works such as encyclopedias and dictionaries on Islam.

17. Jomier, ibid., p.51.

18. Dashti has an interesting discussion of the jinn on pps. 158f. See also Frieling on pps. 40f.

19. The Concise Dictionary Of Islam, ibid., 229; Jomier, ibid., pp. 59f; Sell, Studies in Islam, ibid., pp.210f; Guillaume, Islam, ibid., p. 13.

20. Encyclopedia Britannica, 15:648;

21. Bell, Richard, Introduction to the Quran, pp. 163f. See also: Bell, Richard, The Origin of Islam In Its Christian Environment, ibid., pp 110f, 139f; Sell, Edward, Studies In Islam, ibid., pp 216f. See also Tisdall and Pfander.

22. The Encyclopedia of Islam, (ed. Eliade), 303f; The International Standard Bible Encyclopedia, 1:219f.

23. See: Sell, Studies In Islam, pp. 219f for details.

24. Guillaume, Islam, pp. 38f; Jeffery, A., "Anti-Christian Literature" (Muslim World, vol. 17,(1927) pp 216-219. Kenneth, Cragg, The Call Of The Minaret, ibid., pp.254-264, 286-291. See also Cragg's work, The House Of Islam.

25. Concise Dictionary Of Islam, pp. 229f; Becker, H., Christianity And Islam, pp. 21f;

26. Richard, Bell, Introduction To The Quran, ibid., p. 141.

27. Encyclopedia Britannica, 12:708.

28. The Concise Dictionary Of Islam, pp. 229-230.

29. ibid., p. 229.

30. Victor, Khalil and Deborah, Khalil, "When Christians Meet Muslims," (Christian Herald, July/August, 1988), p.44).

Appendix I

A word needs to be said about English translations of the Quran.

The Muslim claim that the Arabic of the Quran cannot be translated into English or any other language has led to the absurdity of non-arab Muslims praying and reciting Arabic prayers and verses without having a clue as to what they are saying!

It is also an insult to an entire generation of Arabic scholars who have had no difficulty in translating the Quran whatsoever.

The first English translation of the Quran by Western scholars was by George Sale in 1734.

This was not done again until by Rodwell in 1861, Palmer followed in 1880, Wherry in 1882, Pickthal in 1930, Arberry in 1955, Mercier in 1956 and Dawood in 1974.

Muslim translations of the Quran into English began with Adul Hakim Khan in 1905. Mirza Hairat's translation followed in 1919.

The Ahmadiya sect put one out in 1915. But the last Muslim translation that we know of is that of Yusuf Ali's in 1934.

Since so many English speaking Muslims in the West use Ali's translation, we have followed the numbering of verses which he adopted.

This will cause some confusion as the Quran did not originally have numbered verses. Numbering the verses is a Western idea.

Thus translators do differ in how they number the verses. What is verse 5 in Yusuf Ali's translation may be verse 4 in Pickthal. Arberry does not even number each verse! He numbers paragraphs instead.

If you are looking up a verse reference we have given in this book and you are not using Ali's translation, then look before and after the verse we indicate and you will eventually find it.

We have already warned the reader that such Muslim translators as Yusuf Ali will not hesitate to mistranslate the Arabic text in order to keep the English writer from discovering obvious errors in the Quran. Ali is first of all an apologist for Islam and a translator second.

But Ali does serve a purpose that he never imagined. By his constant footnotes in which he tries to rescue the Quran from its many errors and contradictions, he unwittingly alerts the reader to the presence of these errors and contradictions in the text.

Also, his irrational arguments and his obvious mistranslation of various texts such as the one on the Trinity, lead the reader to become highly suspicious that Ali is desperately trying to hide something. The readers of his translation must be aware of its hidden apologetic agenda.

Appendix II

The Legacy Of Elijah Muhammad

by Prof. Colin P. Akridge[1]

Since Elijah Muhammad was the most well known
leader of what is now called the "Black Muslim
Movement," it is important to understand the background and beliefs of this man who so profoundly
influenced the black community in the United States.

Early Life
Elijah Muhammad was not always known by that
name. He was born into this world on Oct. 10, 1897
under the name of Elijah Poole, the son of Wali and
Marie Poole.

Elijah's father was a Baptist pastor who sought to
raise his children in the Christian faith. But one of his
thirteen children would eventually do everything in his
power to destroy the very Gospel that his father and
mother had always loved and preached. This erring
child was none other than Elijah Poole.

A Fateful Meeting
After moving from his native state of Georgia to
Detroit, Michigan, in 1931 Elijah Poole came under

the influence of a colorful religious teacher by the
name of Wallace D. Fard.

Not much is known about Fard except that he was a
peddler of "African" clothing who claimed to be "a
brother from the East."

Seeking to give his followers an African identity and
pride, he urged them to renounce their birth names and
to adopt Arab names such as Muhammad. He also told
them to dress like the Muslims did in the Middle East.
Of course, he was the one to sell them the robes and
other items they needed.

Under Fard's influence, Elijah renounced the Christian faith of his parents and his birth name. Fard then
gave him the Arab name of Karriem.

The Watchtower And Islam

The source of much of what Fard had to say about the
Christian Church and its doctrines came from the
teachings of the Watchtower Bible and Tract Society,
or, as they are commonly known, the Jehovah's Witnesses.

The Watchtower denied all the essential teachings of
historic Christianity such as the Trinity and went from
house to house proclaiming that Jesus Christ was only
a human prophet and NOT divine in any sense.

The Watchtower's denial of the Trinity and its
reduction of Jesus to mere humanity laid the foundation for Fard to introduce his unique brand of Islam.

Going from house to house using Watchtower literature, Fard tore down his black followers' faith in the
Gospel of Jesus Christ. Then when they were no longer
Christians, he introduced Islam as the next logical step
to get away from Christianity which he mocked as "the
white man's religion."

Fard's plan was simple. He took them from the Watchtower to Islam, from the Bible to the Quran and from Jesus to Muhammad. And the driving force which fueled this process was racism.

Black Racism

Fard taught that the white race was the Devil while the black race was divine. He went so far as to say that black people were gods because they were black!

Despite the obvious absurdity of Fard's teaching, it was appealing to those blacks who keenly felt oppressed and needed a way to rebel against what they identified as "the man." Accepting Fard's religion was one way to strike back at the white man.

Given the horrors and injustices that black people have suffered under white racism, Fard used black racism as the bait on the hook to draw them into his religion. Of course, he did not bother to tell them that Islam has always been as racist as any white society.

Elijah Takes Over

Wallace D. Fard suddenly disappeared in 1934 and what happened to him remains a mystery. Many think that he was murdered to get him out of the way.

But regardless of why or how he disappeared, this gave Elijah the perfect opportunity to take over the black Muslim movement. It was at this time that his name was changed to Muhammad instead of Karriem.

Under Elijah's guidance, the movement would grow and become wealthy beyond his wildest dreams. This was due to the natural genius and organizational skills of Elijah Muhammad who went so far as to repay his master by proclaiming that Fard was divine!

Basic Teachings

The basic beliefs of black Muslims are found in Elijah Muhammad's two books, *The Supreme Wisdom* and *The Message To The Black Man In America.*

On God

According to Elijah Muhammad, God is a man and that man was none other than Wallace D. Fard! He stated that Wallace Fard was Allah in human form!

The Christian doctrine of the invisibility and spiritual nature of God was a lie invented by an evil black scientist by the name of YaKub. God was a man and not some kind of Christian "spook" according to Elijah.

Elijah followed Fard's example in using Jehovah's Witness' magazines and books for his arguments against the Trinity, the deity of Christ, etc.

It is interesting to note that some modern Arab Muslim apologists are now using Watchtower literature in their attacks on Christianity.

On The Bible

Elijah did not have much respect for the Bible. He warned his followers that the Bible was pure "poison" because it had been corrupted by the white man. The Quran was far superior. He went so far as to call the Bible a "graveyard of the black man" because it was used by white people to keep him down.

On Jesus

Jesus was only a man and the Arab prophet Muhammad was superior to him in many ways. People should no longer look to a "dead" Jesus according to Elijah.

On Mankind

Elijah continued Fard's racism by teaching that the black race was the first and the last, the Creator of the universe, and the origin of all other races. Black people were actually gods.

On the other hand, white people were not created by Allah. Once again it was that evil black scientist by the name of YaKub who made the white man. He spent six hundred years creating him. Thus white people are devils and not really human beings at all.

Death And The Afterlife

Using Jehovah's Witness theology, Elijah denied that people went to heaven or hell at death. He taught the Watchtower concept of "soul sleep."

On The End Of The World

Following the Watchtower literature which proclaimed 1914 as the "beginning of the end," Elijah twisted it to mean that 1914 signaled the end of the white man's rule and the beginning of black power.

Elijah Muhammad went on to prophesy that Allah would personally intervene in 1970 by destroying the white man and putting black people in control of the world.

The obvious failure of "Allah" to intervene in 1970 as predicted by Elijah is a tremendous embarrassment to black Muslims today. This false prophecy totally destroys any attempt to view him as a "prophet."

The other serious embarrassment of the black Muslim movement in America was the murder of Malcom X.

Malcom X

The son of yet another black Baptist pastor, Malcom

Little converted to the teachings of Elijah Muhammad. Elijah himself changed Little's name to that of Malcom X.

After twelve years of devoted service to the Nation Of Islam, Malcom woke up to the moral problems, greed, jealousy and strife which filled Elijah Muhammad's life. These things began to bother him. How could Elijah be sent from Allah and do all the evil things he was doing?

But it was during his pilgrimage to Mecca that for the first time he clearly saw the heretical and racist nature of the black Muslim movement in America. They were not Muslims at all. The whole thing was a sham.

After much soul searching, he publicly renounced the teachings of W. D. Fard and Elijah Muhammad and began to warn the black community about the racist and heretical nature of the Nation Of Islam. He also warned people that he might be murdered for his courageous stand.

This action by someone so well known in the movement and in the black community at large could not be overlooked. A black Muslim death squad assassinated Malcom X in a public dance hall on Feb. 22, 1965.

But the damage had already been done. The movement fell apart and has fractured into many warring sects.

Elijah's Death
Elijah Muhammad died in 1975. The black Muslim movement in America has since been condemned as heretical by orthodox Islam.

In the end, it must be viewed as just one more indigenous American cult like the Jehovah's Witnesses or the Mormons.

Conclusion

What was the legacy of Elijah Muhammad? It was one of deception, fraud, racism, greed, immorality and murder.

He did not raise the black man to new heights or give him the dignity he needs. Elijah's attempt to fight white racism with black racism only compounded the problem.

And his rejection of the Gospel was actually the rejection of the only way for all people regardless of color to find true dignity.

Footnotes

1. Prof. Akridge is a black scholar in the field of comparative religions with a special emphasis on American cults and sects. It is our pleasure to have him share his many years of research on the black Muslim movement in America.

Bibliography

Carl, F. Ellis Jr., *Beyond Liberation*, (InterVarsity Press, Downers Grove, 1983).

E. U., Essien-Udom, *Black Nationalism*, (Dell Pub., N.Y., 1962)

Peter, Goldman, *The Death and Life Of Malcom X*,

(Harper & Row, N.Y., 1974)

C. Eric, Lincoln, *The Black Muslim In America*, (Beacon Press, Boston, 1973)

Elijah, Muhammad, *The Message To The Black Man In America*, (Muhammad Mosque, Chicago, 1965)

----------------, *Supreme Wisdom*, (Muhammad Mosque, Chicago, n.d.)

Malcom, X, *Autobiography of Malcom X*, (Grove Press, N.Y., 1964)

Bibliography

Selim Abdul-Ahad and W. Gairdner, *The Gospel Of
    Barnabas: An Inquiry*, (Henry Martyn
    Institute Of Islamic Studies, Hyderbad,
    India, 1985).

Ghiyathuddin, Adelphi, and Ernest, Hahn, *The Integrity
    Of The Bible According To The Quran And The
    Hadith*, (Henry Martyn Institute Of Islamic
    Studies, Hyderbad, India, 1977).

Frank, Albright and Richard Bowen, *Archeological
    Discoveries In South Arabia*, (Baltimore, 1958)

Michael, Nazar-Ali, *Islam: A Christian Perspective*,
    (The Westminster Press, Phil., 1983).

Maulna, Muhammad, Ali, *A Manual Of Hadith*, (The
    Ahmadyya Anjuman Ishaat Islam, Lahore,
    n.d.).

Yusuf, Ali, *The Holy Quran*, (Amana Corp., Brentwood,
    Maryland, 1983).

Approaches To Islam In Religious Studies, ed.
    Richard,Martin, (University of Arizona Press,
    Tucson, 1985).

Arthur, J., Arberry, *The Koran*, (Oxford UniversityPress,
    Oxford, 1989).

Ulfat, Aziz-us-samad, *Islam And Christianity*, (Begum
    Aisha Bawany Waqf, Karachi, 1970)

Giullo, Basetti-Sani, *The Koran In The Light Of Christ*,
    (Fransican Herald Press, Chicago, 1977).

N. J., Dawood, *The Koran: Translated with Notes*,
    (Peguin Books, Baltimore,, 1974.

J. H. Bavinck, *The Church Between The Temple And The
    Mosque*, (Wm. B. Eerdmans Pub. Co., Grand
    Rapids, n.d.)

Carl, Becker, *Christianity And Islam*, (Harper & Row,

N.Y., 1909).

Richard, Bell, *Bell's Introduction To The Quran*, Edinburgh University Press, Edinburgh, 1953).

------------, *The Origin Of Islam In Its Christian Environment*, (MacMillan, London, 1926).

M., Bravmann, *The Spiritual Background Of Early Islam*, (E. J. Brill, Leiden, 1972).

Essad, Bey, Moham-med, (Longman, Green & Co., N.Y., 1936).

David, Brown, *The Cross Of The Messiah*, (Sheldon Press, London, 1969).

John, Burton, *The Collection Of The Quran*, (Cambridge University Press, London, 1977).

William Campbell, *The Gospel Of Barnabas: Its True Value*, (Christian Study Center, Rawalpinidi, Pakistan, 1989).

Christian Witness Among Muslims, (Henry Martyn Institute Of Islamic Studies, Hyderbad, India, 1987).

The Concise Encyclopedia Of Islam, ed. Cyril Classe, (Stacey Inter., London, 1989).

Controversial Tracts On Christianity And Mahometanism By The Late Rev. Henry Martyn, ed. Samuel, Lee, (J. Smith, Cambridge, 1824).

Kenneth Cragg, *The Call Of The Minaret*, (Oxford University Press, N.Y., 1956).

------------, *The Event Of The Quran*, (Allen and Unwin, London, 1971).

------------, *The House Of Islam*, (Dickenson, Belmont, Ca., 1969).

------------, *The Mind Of The Quran*, (George Allen and Unwin Ltd., London, 1973).

-------------, *Sandals At The Mosque: Christian Presence Amid Islam*, (Oxford University Press., N.Y., 1959).

Norman, Daniel, *Islam And The West*, (Edinburgh University Press, Edinburgh, 1966).

Ali, Dashti, *23 Years: A Study Of The Prophetic Career Of Mohammed*, (George Allen & Unwin, London, 1985).

El Dessuky, *A Short History Of The Life Of The Prophet Muhammad*, (Uganda Pub. House, Kampala, 1971).

R.F., Dibble, *Mohammed*, (The Viking Press, N.Y., 1926).

James, Dretke, *A Christian Approach To Muslims*, (William Carey Library, London, 1979).

Early Islam, ed. Desmond Stewart, (Time, Inc., N.Y., 1967).

The Encyclopedia Britannica, (Encyclopedia Britannica, Inc., London, 1957).

The Encyclopedia Of Islam, ed. Gibb, Levi-Provencal, Schacht, (E.J. Brill, Leiden, 1960).

The Encyclopedia Of Islam, ed. Houtsma, Arnold, Basset, Hartman, (E.J. Brill, Leiden, 1913.)

The Encyclopedia Of Religion, ed. Mercea Eliade, (MacMillan Pub. Co., N.Y., 1987).

The Encyclopedia of Religion, ed. Paul Meagher, Thomas O'Brain, Consuela Aherne, (Corpus Pub., Washington, D.C., 1979).

The Encyclopedia Of Religion and Ethics, ed. James Hastings, (T&T Clark, Edinburgh, 1908)

The Facts On File: Encyclopedia of World Mythology and Legend, ed. Anthony Mercatane, Facts Of File, N.Y., 1983).

Caesar, Farah, *Islam: Beliefs and Observations*,
        (Barrons, N.Y., 1987).
Sydney, Fisher, *The Middle East: A History*, (Alfred
        Knopf, N.Y., 1969).
Rudolph, Frieling, *Christianity And Islam: A Battle For
        The True Image Of Man*, (Floris Books,
        Edinburgh, 1978).
C. George, Fry and James, King, *Islam: A Survey Of
        The Muslim Faith*, (Baker, Grand Rapids,
        1980).
Helmut, Gatje, *The Quran And Its Exegesis*, (University
        of California Press, L.A., 1976).
John, Gilchrist, *Christ In Islam And Christianity*, (Jesus
        To The Muslims, Benoni, South Africa, 1987)
---------------, *The Crucifixion Of Christ: A Fact, Not
        Fiction*, (Jesus To The Muslims, Benoni, South
        Africa, 1987).
---------------, *Is Muhammad Foretold In The Bible?*,
        (Jesus To The Muslims, Benoni, South Africa,
        1987).
---------------, *Jam' Al-Qur'an: The Codification Of The
        Quran Text*, (Jesus To The Muslims, Benoni,
        South Africa, 1989).
---------------, *Origins and Sources Of The Gospel Of
        Barnabas*, (Jesus To The Muslims, Benoni,
        South Africa, 1987).
---------------, *The Textual History Of The Quran And The
        Bible*, (Jesus To The Muslims, Benoni, South
        Africa, 1987).
---------------, *What Indeed Was The Sign Of Jonah?*,
        (Jesus To The Muslims, Benoni, South Africa,
        1987).
H. A. R. , Gibb, *Mohammedanism: An Historical Survey*,
        (Mentor Books, N.Y., 1955).

-----------,"*Pre-Islamic Monotheism in Arabia*"," (Harvard Theological Review, vol. 55, 1962.

John, Glubb, *The Life And Times Of Muhammad*, (Stein and Day, N.Y., 1970).

Martin, Goldsmith, *Islam And Christian Witness*, (InterVarsity Press, Downers Grove, Ill., 1982).

Alfred, Guillaume, *Islam*, (Penguin Books, London, 1954)

-----------------, *New Light On The Life Of Muhammad*, (Manchester University Press, Manchester, n.d.).

-----------------, *The Traditions Of Islam*, (Clarendon Press, London, 1924)

Ernest, Hahn, Jesus In Islam, (Henry Martyn Institute Of Islamic Studies, Hyderbad, India, 1987).

------------, *Understanding Some Muslims Misunderstandings*, (Fellowship Of Faith, Toronto, 1983).

Abdul, Hamed, *Islam and Christianity*, (Carlton Press, N.Y., 1967).

Mahmoud, Hoballah, *Muhammad The Prophet*, (The Islamic Center, Washington, D. C., n.d.).

Muhammad, Husayn, Haykal, *The Life Of Muhammad*, (Crescent Pub. Co., Delhi, 1976).

Thomas, Hughes, *A Dictionary of Islam*, (Allen & Co., London, 1885).

Muhammed, Hamidullah, *Introduction To Islam*, (Centre Culturel Islamique, Paris, 1957).

C., Hurgronji, *Mohammedanism*, (Hyperion Press, Westport, Conn., 1981).

Internationl Journal Of Middle East Studies.

International Journal Of Islamic and Arabic Studies.

Ibraham, Ishak, *Black Gold And Holy War*, (Thomas

Nelson, Nasville, 1983)

Islam And Christianity; Or, The Quran And The Bible; A Letter To A Muslim Friend, By A Missionary, (American Tract Society, N.Y., 1901)

Islam: The First & Final Religion, (Begum Aisha Bawany Waqf, Karachi, 1978).

Toshihikio, Izutsu, Ethico-religious Concepts On The Quran, (McGill University Press, Montreal, 1966).

Arthur, Jeffery, *"Anti-Christian Literature,"* (Muslim World, vol. 17, 1927.

--------------, *The Foreign Vocabulary Of The Quran,* (Baroda: Oriental Institute, 1938)

--------------, ed. *Islam: Muhammad and His Religion,* (The Liberal Arts Press, N.Y., 1958).

--------------, *Materials For The History Of The Text Of The Quran,* (E.J. Brill, Leiden, 1937)

--------------, *The Quran As Scripture,* (Russell F. Moore, N.Y., 1952).

Jasques, Jomier, The Bible And The Quran, (Henry Regency Co., Chicago, 1959).

Journal of Semetic Studies. Abraham, Katsh, Judaism In Islam: Biblical and Talmudic Backgrounds Of The Koran and Its Commentaries, (New York University Press, N.Y., 1954).

Badru, Kateregga and David, Shenk, *Islam And Christianity,* (Wm. B., Eerdmans Pub. Co., Grand Rapids, 1980).

Muhammad, Kutub, *Islam: The Misunderstood Religion,* (International Islamic Federation Of Student Organizations, Kuwait, 1982).

Abdul, Mandudi, *The Meaning Of The Quran,* (Islamic Pub. Ltd., Lahore, 1967).

C. R. Marsh, *Share Your Faith With A Muslim*, (Moody Press, Chicago, 1975).

John, McClintock and James Strong, *Cyclopedia Of Biblical, Theological, and Ecclesiastical Literature*, (Baker, Grand Rapids, 1981).

Josh, McDowell and John, Gilchrist, *The Islam Debate*, (Here's Life Pub., San Berndino, Ca., 1983).

Henry, Mercier, *The Koran*, (Luzac & Co., London, 1956).

William, Miller, *A Christian's Response To Islam*, (Pres. & Ref. Pub. Co., Phillipsburg, N. J., 1976).

G.E., Morrison, *The Christian Approach To The Muslim*, (Edinburgh House Press, London, 1959).

William, Muir, *The Life Of Mohammed From Original Sources*, (John Grant, London, 1923).

-------------, *Some Of The Sources Of The Coran*, (n.p., London, 1901).

Muslim-Christian Conflicts, ed. Saud, Joseph and Barbara, Pillsbury, (Western Press, Boulder, Col., 1978).

Kausar, Nizar, *Islam & The West*, (Muhammad Ashraf, Karachi, 1976).

Phil, Parshall, *Bridges To Islam*, (Baker, Grand Rapids, 1985)

John, Penrice, *A Dictionary And Glossary Of The Koran*, (Biblo and Tanner, N.Y., 1969).

C., Pfander, *Balance Of Truth*, (The Religious Tract Society, London, 1910).

Marmaduke, Pickthall, *The Meaning Of The Glorious Koran*, (New American Library, N.Y., n.d.)

Sayyid, Qutb, *Islam: The Religion Of The Future*, (International Islamic Federation of Student Organizations, Kuwait, n.d.).

------------, *This Religion Of Islam*, (International Islamic Federation Of Student Organizations, Kuwait, 1982).

Cannon, Sell and David Maroliouth, *"Christ In Mohammedan Literature,"* in James, Hastings, ed., Dictionary Of Christ And The Gospels, (Charles Scribners' Sons, N.Y., 1917)

Cannon, Sell, *Historical Development Of The Quran*, (Diocesan Press, Madras, 1923).

------------, *The Life Of Muhammad*, (Christian Literature Society Of India, Lahore, 1913).

------------, *Studies In Islam*, (Diocesan Press, London, 1928). M.S., Seale, Quran and Bible, (Croom Helm, London, 1978).

Shorter Encyclopedia Of Islam, ed. H. Gibb and J. Kramers, (Cornell University Press, Ithica, N.Y., 1953).

Anis, Shorrosh, *Islam Revealed*, (Thomas Nelson Pub., Nashville, 1988).

Henry, Preserved, Smith, *The Bible and Islam; Or, The Influence Of The Old and New Testaments On The Religion Of Mohammed*, (Charles Scribners' Sons, N. Y., 1897).

Salomon, Reinach, *Orpheus: A History Of Religion*, (Liveright, Inc., N.Y., 1932).

Jane, Smith, *An Historical and Semetic Study Of The Term Islam As Seen In A Sequence of Quran Commentaries*, (University of Montana for Harvard University dissertations, 1970).

Percy, Smith, *"Did Jesus Foretell Amed?"*, (Muslim World, vol. 12, 1922.

H., Spencer, *Islam and The Gospel Of God*, (S.P.C.K., Madras, 1956)

Henry, Stanton, *The Teaching Of The Quran*, (Biblo and
    Tanner, N.Y., 1969).

James, Sweetman, *The Bible In Islam*, (British & Foreign
    Society, London, 1953).

William, Tisdall, *A Manual Of The Leading
    Muhammadan Objections To Objections to
    Christianity*, (S.P.C.K., London, 1911).

---------------, *Original Sources Of Islam*, (T. & T. Clark,
    Edinburgh, 1901).

---------------, *The Religion Of The Crescent; Being The
    James Long Lectures On Muhammadanism*,
    (S.P.C.K., London, 1910).

W. Montgomery, Watt, *Companion To The Quran*,
    (George Allen & Unwin Ltd., London, 1967).

------------------, "Belief In a "High God" In Pre-Islamic
    Mecca,", (*Journal Of Semitic Studies*, vol. 16,
    1971).

------------------, *Muhammad At Mecca*, (Clarendon
    Press, Oxford, 1953).

------------------, *Muhammad At Medina*, (Clarendon
    Press, Oxford, 1956).

E. M., Wherry, *A Comprehensive Commentary On The
    Quran*, (Otto Zeller Verlag, Osnabruck, 1973).

Edward, Westermarck, *Pagan Survivals in Mohammedan
    Civilization*, (Philo Press, Amsterdam, 1933).

Don, Wismer, *The Islamic Jesus*, (Garland Pub., N.Y.,
    1977).

Samuel, Zwemer, Across *The World of Islam: Studies In
    Aspects Of The Mohammedan Faith And In The
    Present Awaking Of The Moslem Multitudes*,
    (Fleming Revell, N.Y., 1929).

------------, *The Cross Above The Crescent*, (Zondervan
    Pub. Co., Grand Rapids, 1941).

------------, *Islam: A Challenge To Faith*, (Student
Volunteer Movement For Foreign Missions,
N.Y., 1908).

------------, *The Moslem Doctrines Of God; An Essay On
The Character And Attributes Of Allah
According To The Koran*, (American Tract
Society, N.Y., 1905).

Index